Richard W. Gibford

TROUT FLIES IN NEW ZEALAND

By the same author:

MR HUNDRED PER CENT
FRED FLETCHER'S TAUPO TALES

TROUT FLIES IN NEW ZEALAND

by

KEITH DRAPER

A. H. & A. W. REED
Wellington Auckland Christchurch
Sydney Melbourne

First published 1971

A. H. & A. W. REED LTD.
182 Wakefield Street, Wellington
29 Dacre Street, Auckland
165 Cashel Street, Christchurch
51 Whiting Street, Artarmon, Sydney
357 Little Collins Street, Melbourne

© 1971   KEITH DRAPER

ISBN: 0 589 00655 x

This book is copyright. Except for purposes of private study, criticism or review, no part may be reproduced by any process including stencilling or photocopying without the prior written permission of the publisher.

Set by Typemasters Ltd, Auckland.
Printed by Dai Nippon Printing Co. (International) Ltd., Hong Kong.

DEDICATION

*In grateful tribute to
the pioneers of trout
acclimatisation in New Zealand.*

CONTENTS

FOREWORD	11
INTRODUCTION	13
ENTOMOLOGY	
Beetles, caddis flies, cicadas, dragonflies, ephemeroptera (mayflies) flies, freshwater crayfish, freshwater snails, ichneumon flies lace-wings, midges, minnows, shrimps, stone flies	17
LURES	41
WET AND DRY FLIES	93
NYMPHS	159
APPENDIX 1	174
APPENDIX 2	175
APPENDIX 3	177
BIBLIOGRAPHY	178
GLOSSARY OF TERMS	179

LIST OF COLOUR PLATES

PLATE 1
    Taupo and Rotorua lures..   84

PLATE 2
    Night lures, Canterbury lures,
    smelt flies, fur flies, and specials   86

PLATE 3
    Wet flies and Nymphs   88

PLATE 4
    Dry flies, some old favourite and
    many new patterns   90

ACKNOWLEDGMENTS

This book is the result of the kind and generous help of many anglers. All at some time or other gave willingly of their knowledge, some of them never knowing that their valued opinions would ever be recorded. Besides information, some supplied fly specimens which I highly value.

I must make special mention of the time and effort spent by Robert K. Bragg of Christchurch, who went to a great deal of trouble in locating the origins of many South Island patterns. He also tied a good many specimens for me. He is a professional fly-dresser, and they are an excellent testimony to the quality of his craftsmanship. He put himself to a great deal of work because, like myself, he believes it only right that the correct origins of fly patterns should be recorded. Unfortunately many have already been lost, but perhaps some readers can oblige me with more information for the record.

Others who helped me are:

J. B. Bockett of Taupo, who loaned me Captain Hamilton's book, *Trout Fishing and Sport in Maoriland*.

E. Bosomworth of Rotorua, W. Broad of Wellington, J. Cockburn of Hatepe, Taupo, who supplied me with patterns and samples.

P. Cullen of Gore, for information which led to the tracking down of several patterns.

The late D. A. (Peter) Dawson of Hastings, who first showed me how to dry fly-fish successfully.

A. Duncum of Napier for his information on several patterns.

N. Feierabend of Dannevirke for information.

The late Fred Fletcher of Taupo, for his encouragement and help in the early stages of preparation.

W. Gibb of Lower Hutt, for his information on the Mataura patterns.

G. Goulter of Wanganui, who readily passed on information on the waters he has successfully angled.

W. Hamill of Rotorua, for information on patterns.

O. S. Hintz of Taupo, for his information on patterns, and the fine specimen of a Parson's Glory he tied in the manner in which its creator originally laid down.

G. C. Kelly of Taupo, for his encouragement and help with patterns.

A. V. (Bruno) Kemball of Hatepe, Taupo, who is prepared to share his knowledge with anyone who calls at his fly and tackle shop.

W. S. C. Laurie of Auckland, for the samples of the late Jimmy Morris's flies and the accompanying notes that went with them.

P. Laing of Christchurch, for information and fly specimens — fine examples of an amateur tier's skill.

F. Lord of Rotorua, for his anecdotes on the origins of several patterns.

S. (Syd) Moor of the Zoology Department, Victoria University, for identifying natural specimens for my collection.

The late Hiini Northcroft of Taupo, for allowing me to inspect the fly boxes of the late W. Branson, wherein I found among other patterns, a Red Hackle, as described by Captain G. D. Hamilton. (This fly is shown in the coloured plates.)

H. A. (Tony) Orman of Havelock North, for information on patterns.

G. Sanderson of Turangi, for information on patterns.

N. Thomas of Temuka, for the copy of the Teuka fly.

A. Ware of Kaiangaroa for his opinions on patterns.

J. Wells Snr. of Rotorua, for his information on the Kilwell range of flies.

W. Willis of Te Kuiti, for his information on patterns and the samples he dressed.

To complete this extensive list I wish to thank my wife Margaret for the patient help in making up and typing the script from a seemingly unrelated heap of untidy notes, and my editor, David Elworthy, for his aid and practical suggestions as a keen fellow angler.

FOREWORD

In Keith Draper's book we have, at last, the New Zealand fly fisherman's entomology in full text and with coloured plates showing the practical representations of our river and lake trout food.

This is a remarkable book. Mr Draper is not only a keen angler, but also a naturalist and artist. His drawings of the naturals are the work of a skilled draftsman who has a thorough acquaintance with his subjects.

It is the fly, however, which is the chief concern of the author. In this field he offers the New Zealand angler a rich fund of knowledge. Not only is there a large selection of proven catchers, but a detailed list of the materials used in their tying. Most of the flies and lures illustrated are the author's own dressings.

Draper himself is a man of the open. He works tirelessly for the preservation of clear air, pure streams and fair play. His book, to which it is my happy privilege to write the foreword, will be a cherished guide and companion for the New Zealand anglers for many years.

Greg Kelly

INTRODUCTION

Early New Zealand settlers were fly fishing long before the introduction of trout to New Zealand. The native grayling (*Prototroctes Oxyrhynchus*, upokororo to the Maoris) abounded in the clear freshwater streams and readily took the fly.

W. J. Phillips in *Native Fishes*, tells of one early Taranaki angler whose diary records taking 1,152 grayling in fifty-eight fishing days. Alas — the grayling, like the moa, has gone. Many blame the introduction of trout, combined with extensive bush felling and farm development, for their demise, and it is sad to think that what must have been an excellent indigenous fly fish has disappeared. I recall my maternal grandfather telling of fishing for them in the lower Wairarapa in his boyhood. This would have been in the 1880s or 90s.

Anglers then have been fly fishing in New Zealand for well over a century, and for many years the flies found in their boxes were the flies being used by trout fishermen in the United Kingdom.

The trout flies of England, Scotland, Ireland and Wales have been used with success the world over wherever trout live. Combined with their larger English cousins, the sea trout and salmon flies, they have formed a base for the development of the New Zealand trout fly. Some of them are still in use today, their origins lost in antiquity. The March Brown, Red Palmer and Hare's Ear are among these grand old favourites, and little can be done to improve on the original patterns.

Wet and dry flies have mainly followed the traditional manner of dressing. In my investigations before writing this work, I found that all over the country individuals had been working on their own, studying basic entomology, tying their own patterns and using them with success. Most of them were individualists, a little on the reticent side but always willing to help anyone who showed an intelligent interest in the advanced technicalities of trout fishing. From these investigations some interesting patterns have come to light. I hope some of my readers will profit from their discovery and advance their knowledge of streamside tactics.

A fish that is feeding selectively is a challenge. An angler's skill and knowledge is tested and if he takes his quarry on a delicate fly which he has tied himself, his satisfaction is complete. The rewards of fly fishing are very personal and in all truth each man is his own judge. This has been the case ever since men went fishing not because they needed fish for the table, but because they enjoyed it.!

Fly fishermen the world over have an ancient heritage ,and while most of us have never floated a fly down a chalk stream, fished a team of wets on a tumbled north country beck, or swum a salmon fly through a highland pool, those faraway places are the cradles of our art. I have always been proud to be a fourth generation New Zealander, but I am very aware of the debt we owe to our British heritage, rich in angling lore and literature.

This book then is an attempt to record as well as I am able a list of flies used in New Zealand. I have no doubt it is incomplete and that some anglers will be disappointed to see their own favourite missing. In consolation I hope I may have introduced them to some new patterns. Just as some of the flies I have recorded here are now almost obsolete, no doubt in another generation many of today's favourites will have been replaced by another breed of new creations.

Some people will also disagree with a number of the dressings. This will not surprise me as I have often disagreed myself. That is the way it is. What I have written here is honestly recorded in an attempt to catalogue the history of our country's trout flies and lures, their dressings and their use.

Three chapters list the three different types of fly by name, and in alphabetical sequence in each case lures, lake and big-river flies which usually represent small fish; wet and dry flies, which represent insects, and nymphs, which represent the larva stage of insects.

1

ENTOMOLOGY FOR THE ANGLER

Dealing with basic entomology and a description of some of the creatures upon which trout prey, and the artificial lures and flies designed to copy them.

To be a successful stream angler one must have at least a working knowledge of entomology, the cycles of the various insects and the habits of the quarry. This is not difficult to achieve. There are several small books and booklets on the subject which can be a great help in identifying the insect groups. Identify only one insect, read of its habits and a whole new facet of angling will open up before you, with yet another fascinating step waiting to be discovered, perhaps on your next streamside visit.

Autopsies of the trout you catch will provide you with plenty of insects for subsequent identification and tell you what the trout was feeding on. You will know what time of day it was taken and there in lies yet another clue.

Experience will show what flies will be taken when selective trout are on the feed, and that often a pattern that will be accepted will bear no discernible likeness to the natural they were feeding on at the time. Of course there are days when the fish are taking everything and anything. An autopsy on an eighteen-inch brown trout I took on the Waipunga one January evening in 1967 showed that he had started off his afternoon with one of his young brothers about five inches long. Then he began on cicadas until he was really stuffed. Mixed with these were tiger beetles and longhorn pinus beatles, a couple of green beetles, and one blowfly. He had then started on a fall of umber spinners (*Coloburiscus humeralis*) when he took my Coch-y-bondhu. . . . Theoretically that trout should have taken anything from a stream fly through to a dry spinner.

Small delicate flies are becoming more popular as anglers realise that trout will take a No. 16 or 18 where they refuse the number 10 or 12 which the angler has used for a good many years.

In fact I firmly believe that size can often be the more critical reason for a fish accepting or refusing a fly. Some shops still demand and sell green beetle flies tied on No. 8 hooks when a size 14 much more closely resembles the natural. The same applies to dry flies and most rising nymphs. There will always be occasions when a large fly will take fish, but when trout become too critical, it is often wise to change to smaller sizes rather than change patterns. This is becoming increasingly evident as angling pressure on the streams results in an educated strain of trout well schooled in resisting the temptation to take larger flies.

But it is a problem in New Zealand to procure flies in sizes 16 and 18. They are to be found in some shops, but the demand is not yet great enough, and as they are both time-consuming and exacting to make a good dry fly of this size is expensive to buy. Also due to a world shortage of prime cock-necks and the ever-increasing price of those available, the dry fly angler must be prepared to pay for quality.

The alternative is for him to make his own, and provided he can discipline his fingers he will find himself engrossed in as fascinating a hobby as ever there was.

The following chapters are intended to give the reader a basic understanding of the type of rudimentary natural history with which an angler should acquaint himself. If it appears that too much attention is given to long-winded scientific names I do not apologise, as it is only by positive identification that some species can be identified. Individual species often do not have a common name, so the scientific name has to be used. This is not intended as a pretentious display, and anglers sufficiently advanced in their art will realise this.

BEETLES (COLEOPTERA)
Green and Brown

These two common insects are of great interest to the fly fisherman and it is during the "hatches" of beetles that the dry fly angler can be assured of enjoying good sport. While the brown beetle (*Odontria*) usually begins to appear about late October or November and swarms for six weeks or so, I have noticed odd specimens at all times of the year. In fact I have a note of a warm wet front that passed

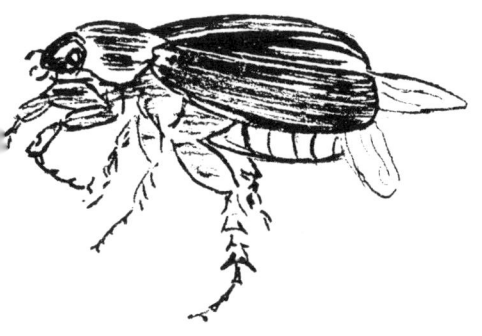

Brown beetle, side view, *Costelytra zealandica*, ½ in long.

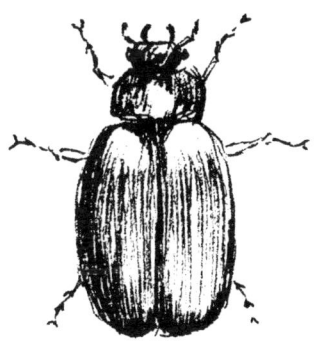

Dorsal view of the brown beetle.

Brown beetle in flight.

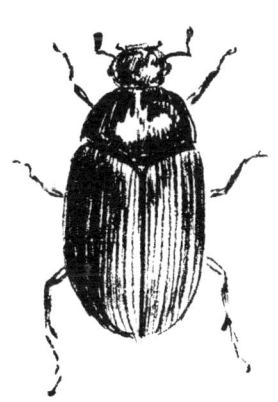

Green manuka beetle, *Pyronota festiva*.

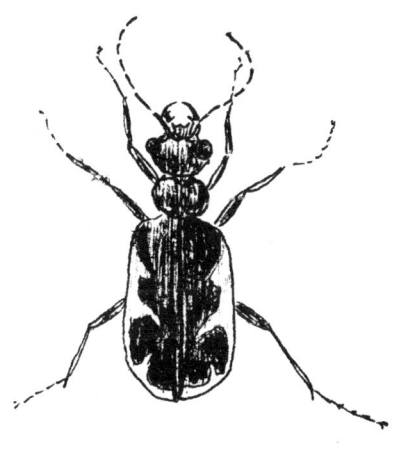

Tiger beetle, *Nescicindella tuperaulata*, ½ in long.

over the centre of the North Island on 24 May 1967, resulting in a swarm of beetles that night.

The green beetle (*Pyronota festivica*) is a close relative of the brown, and anglers are familiar with the clusters of them that hang on the manuka bushes along the stream-edges. In fact they form a principal item of diet for back-country trout. I have seen the Waikato river covered with rising trout as an equinoctial wind blew the insects on to the water. As both beetles have a similar silhouette, a single fly can be used whenever trout are rising to either species, although the green beetle is smaller than the brown. A Coch-y-bondhu is as good a fly as any I know when trout are feeding on these beetles, while some anglers swear by a Red Palmer.

There is an increasing demand, however, for flies tied to look more like the beetles themselves, although it is difficult to get these patterns to float very effectively. But there can be no doubt that fished on a floating line and handled in the same manner as a nymph they are very effective. Besides these two species there are many other varieties, most of which turn up in autopsies on occasions. The tiger beetle (*Neocicindella tuberculata*) is by far the most common in my experience, but none of the others provide so rich a banquet for the trout as do the green and the brown.

CADDIS, OR SEDGE FLIES (TRICHOPTERA)

The caddis in both its larval and adult forms probably constitutes the main item of food on all New Zealand trout streams. This is the case the world over, and all anglers are familiar with the various species. They are easily identified in the larval form. Their little grublike bodies are encased in structures which vary according to the species. Some of the more common are the horny-cased, with their smooth curved-horn-shaped houses.

Next there is the sandy-cased caddis, which is found nearly everywhere. Its house is shaped in much the same manner as the horny-cased, except that it is made of tiny grains of sand cemented together. Again there is another species which builds its house of sand grains constructed in spiral form, similar to a snail shell.

Another is the stick caddis, which utilises a piece of hollow straw or some other such material. Another builds a small net among the stones and feeds on the minute plant and animal matter swept along by the stream current. Yet another species, one of the largest, creeps around under the rocks and is carnivorous.

There will not be a stream fisherman who hasn't found a trout's stomach crammed with these insects at some time or other. A small lightly dressed dull-coloured nymph fished along the bottom is perhaps the deadliest way of catching these bottom feeders.

When the time is right the larvae pupate in various types of cocoon and later crawl or swim to the surface where they emerge as adults. The experts tell us that they swim to a rock where they split and hatch, but in some species, such as those found on the Waikato, the fly will appear on the surface and then skitter off to the edge. This is an exciting time for a trout, and either a nymph or a dry fly will be readily taken, with perhaps a preference shown for the former. As the evening grows darker the dry fly comes into favour, and you can fish well into the night if the temperature remains mild.

natural size ½ in

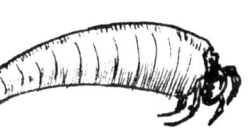

Horn caddis, *Olinga feredayi*

Stick caddis, *Triplectides obsoleta*

Net-building caddis, *Hydropsyche colonica*

Spiral-case caddis, *Helicopsyche*

Sand-cased caddis, *Pycnocentria*

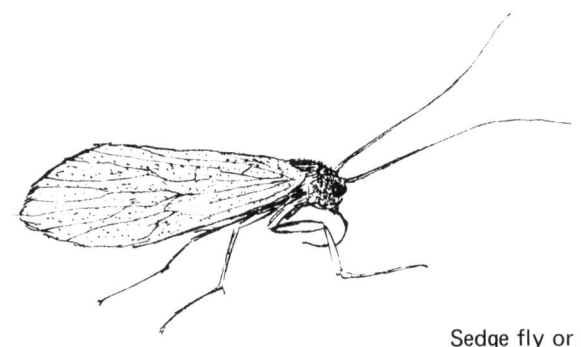

Sedge fly or Caddis fly family, *Trichoptera hydrobiosis*, ⅔ in long.

Sedge fly, *Hydropsyche*, ½ in long.

Dorsal view of sedge fly.

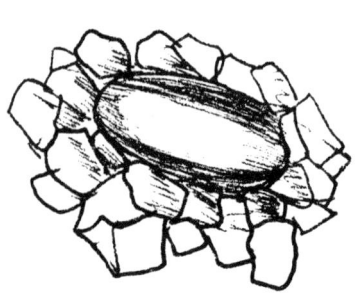

Pupating larva of caddis, *Hydrobiosus*.

A fly favoured by many anglers during the sedge rise is the March Brown. Fished as a dry it tends to be unsuccessful unless its hackle has been well fortified with stiff cock hackles.

The March Brown's success is due to the fact that it is taken for a pupating sedge. It is usually in or just under the surface when fished on dry tackle and is a good fly to use earlier in the evening, although I think a well-hackled sedge fly is more profitable when the light begins to go.

Some of the more popular sedge flies are two New Zealand patterns, Pye's Sedge and Thompson's Moth. Also popular is the Turkey Sedge, as well as the old-world patterns of Ginger Sedge, Dark Sedge, Silver Sedge, and Paragon.

Sedging trout will also take a good many wet patterns, provided these are fished to them in the proper manner. A good example of this is the Twilight Beauty tied with a fairly heavy wing. While fish feed almost exclusively on sedge when they are on the water, autopsies will show that they are not above helping themselves to the odd beetle or anything else that is washed down with the current.

The adult sedge flies have a fairly long life, in some cases several weeks, and during the hours of daylight they will be found under shady banks and among the vegetation. It is in the evening that mating takes place and the female lays her eggs under the water. Some species actually creep under the surface and lay their eggs under the stones. An inspection along the stream edge in the summer will reveal hundreds of these on the undersides of stones. Other species drop their eggs on the surface, while yet another spews out its larvae in live form by the hundred.

The caddis is an uncomplicated insect, and is worthy of the angler's attention as a good subject for streamside study.

CICADAS

There are in New Zealand many species of cicada, or locust as they are often erroneously called. Any angler who has fished a back country stream during summer will know that when the sun is shining their strident chorus is an ever-present background to the chuckle of the stream. Trout cannot resist a cicada and on some days a lot of them seem to end up in the water. I have caught trout that were full of them, almost to the exclusion of all else. Mr Rex Mellsop, an Auckland dry fly fisherman, once told me on a streamside meeting that he always considered the molefly to be the best answer for cicada-inclined fish. Now the molefly is really a progressive form of palmer, which is held in high regard by many anglers as a good summer fly when fishing blind. The Taumaranui professional fly-tier W. Edwards tells me he uses a large heavily hackled Black Palmer tied on a Nc. 6 hook when the large black or bush cicada is is season.

There are many species of cicada in varying sizes and colours, reddy-brown and green being the most common.

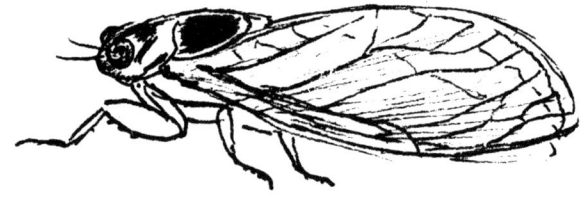

Cicada approximately 1 in long.

DRAGONFLIES AND DAMSEL FLIES (ODONATA)

There is no doubt that in all lakes, especially those with weedy and silty margins, the larvae of dragon and damsel flies form an important part of a trout's diet. Both species are voracious predators. The squat ugly larvae of the dragonfly lurks on the bottom. It has a set of retracting mandibles which dart out to seize any small unsuspecting insect or fish which comes within range. When ready it crawls out of the water and hatches into the adult insect. It then sets off on its hawking flights, still pursuing its carnivorous course.

The nymph of the dragonfly is often copied by using any type of short-tailed lure fished along the bottom. Mrs Simpson and Hamill's Killer are highly regarded for this purpose. Home tiers making their own flies for this purpose often tie in a very short tail of squirrel hair. The best for the purpose is to be found at the butt of the tail, and

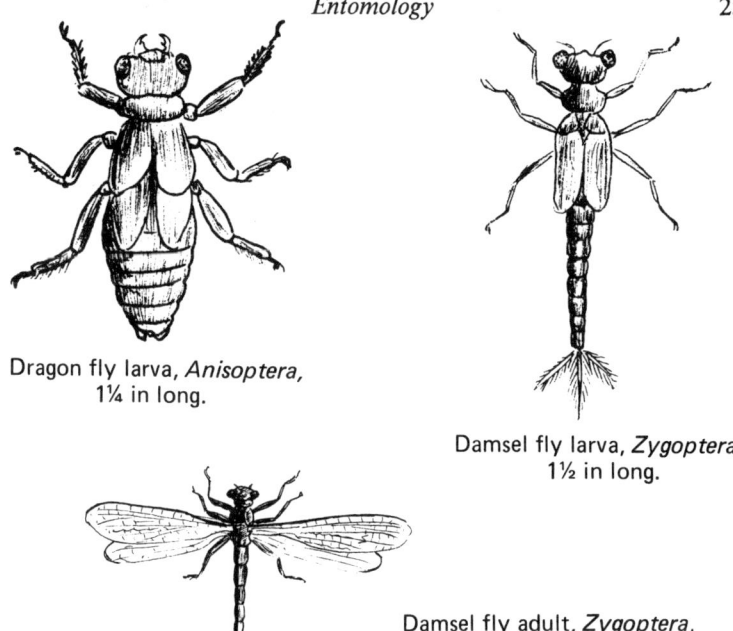

Dragon fly larva, *Anisoptera*, 1¼ in long.

Damsel fly larva, *Zygoptera*, 1½ in long.

Damsel fly adult, *Zygoptera*, 1½ in long.

the ideal length about half that of the hook. The lure should be fished as close as possible to the bottom, being retrieved in short stops and starts.

The nymph of the smaller damsel fly is a more gracefully built creature, but equally as voracious. It lurks among the fronds and stems of water weeds, propelling itself by undulating its slender body from side to side. Several of these were among the creatures captured by my children on a tadpoling expedition and it was a matter of great interest to watch their activities in the acquarium in which they were housed. The nymph would hang inert in the water until an unsuspecting water-boatman came near, when with a couple of swift jerks the damsel nymph would seize it, discarding the unfortunate victim some time later as a whitened and empty husk.

There are several dressings to represent the adult dragon and damsel flies. These are: Tonga, Quill Dragonfly, Danielson's Damsel Fly. Two dressings are given for dragon larvae nymphs and one damsel nymph.

EPHEMEROPTERA (MAYFLIES)

Mayflies embrace over twenty recognised species in New Zealand. There can be no doubt that in the larval form they constitute a significant portion of the trout's diet, particularly in the more stable type of stream rather than rivers with silty flood-scoured beds. Recent studies have shown that in the face of back-country development and the widespread use of insecticides and weed sprays many small stream populations of mayfly have been seriously affected. They appear to be one of the more susceptible species to this ever-growing menace.

Some streams and districts are favoured with good mayfly rises while in others the hatches are sporadic and thin.

The mayfly has always been an item of interest to fly fishermen as it symbolises the gentle aesthetic qualities often associated with trout fishing. The angler's skill is really put to the test in this highly specialised branch of the art of angling. Most New Zealand fly fishermen who have made a close study of their sport are familiar with the literary works stimulated by dry fly angling on the chalk streams of southern England, and the names of Halford and Skues, two high priests of the art, will be familiar. It is perhaps unfortunate, however, that the influence of the chalk stream has been given undue emphasis by many New Zealand dry fly anglers, and while there can be no doubt that there are some streams in this country, especially in the lower portion of the South Island, which afford dry fly angling of a highly specialised order, I feel that on the majority of our streams and rivers the mayfly rise is not as important as is the rise to many insects of terrestrial origins.

The study of this particular group provides a challenge that is not to be found in any other order of insects. The real action begins when the nymphs begin to rise to the surface and the trout start taking their toll. When the nymph reaches the surface the first stage of the adult fly emerges. The entomologist calls this stage a sub-imago and the angler calls it a dun. The dun usually has opaque wings, the veining giving the wing a mottled appearance. The insect leaves the water, usually flying in a clumsy fashion to the nearest undergrowth. It can readily be recognised by the manner in which it flies, the long slender body curling downwards, adorned with long slender whisks, or setae. Depending on the species the time that elapses before the next metamorphosis varies from a period of several hours to a day. The insects have no mouths and cannot feed, so are destined to a short life. Their scientific name is derived from the word "ephemeral".

It seems difficult to believe, but from this fragile-looking insect, yet another emerges. The thorax splits and the mature adult emerges. The insect now has clear sparkling wings, the veining being usually of a dark black or brown. This creature, also fragile is the imago, or spinner as the anglers call it, and during late afternoon it will emerge to begin the mating dance. The insects congregate over the

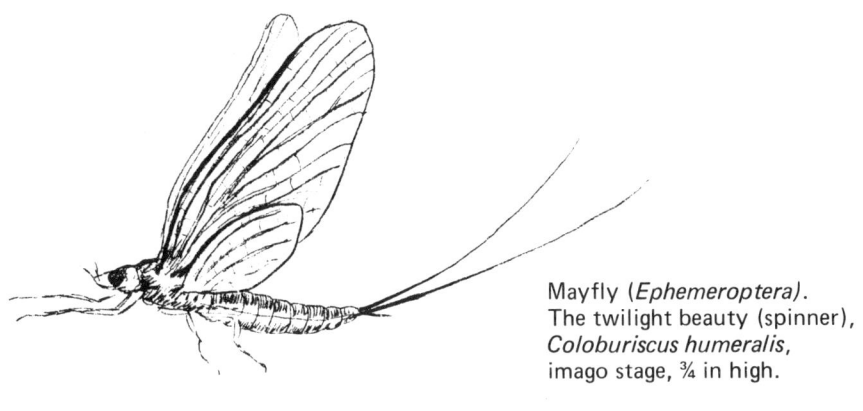

Mayfly (*Ephemeroptera*). The twilight beauty (spinner), *Coloburiscus humeralis*, imago stage, ¾ in high.

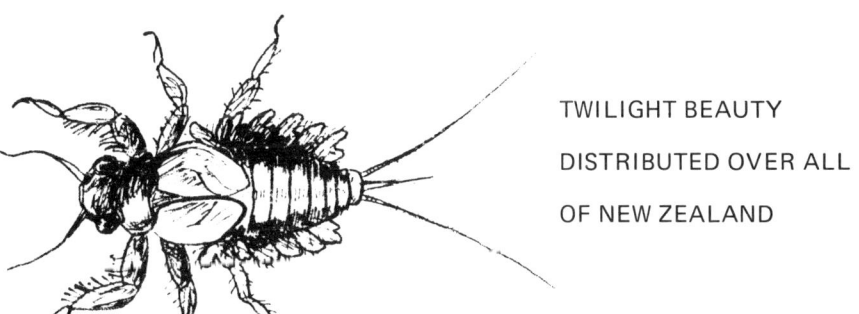

TWILIGHT BEAUTY DISTRIBUTED OVER ALL OF NEW ZEALAND

Mature Nymph of *Coloburiscus humeralis*. The wing pads are nearly complete showing that the nymph is ready to rise and hatch as a dun (sub-imago). Body is ⁷⁄₁₆ in long.

water in swarms, usually flying at a height of six to eight feet. The males rise up and down like so many helicopters; and in many species they have red eyes, as opposed to the more neutral-coloured head on the female.

Suddenly you will see the whole swarm rise swiftly and fly nearly out of sight into the evening sky. Then they will descend and begin their pulsating hovering again. This sudden rise is caused by a female coming out of the bushes and flying swiftly up through the swarm, where she is pursued and eventually seized by one of the males. Fertilised, the female drops down over the water to begin egg-laying.

This is the insect which interests the angler. The mayfly skims above the surface of the pool, touching the surface every few inches as she lays her eggs. Spent, she eventually floats down on the surface inert, her wings outspread, now the spent spinner of the angler.

Briefly, that is the history of a mayfly although there are deviations with some species. For instance I have long suspected that a good many of our New Zealand duns do not hatch in the prescribed manner but crawl out on to the rocks along river margins. Any angler who has not noticed stones with dozens of these nymphal shucks dried upon them has not been using his eyes. I also suspect that some of them hatch at night when the angler is unable to exploit their appearance. I recall waiting one December evening for a sedge hatch to commence. It was nearly ten o'clock and I shone my torch occasionally to see if any sedges were coming off the water or scurrying over the rocks. Suddenly I saw a dun sitting on a stone close by the water's edge. Its wings were pearly white and I carefully took it in my hand while I fumbled for a flybox or something to put it in. When I finally managed to open a lid, it escaped during the attempted transfer. It was, I think, a specimen of *Atalophlebia dentata*.

The matching of an artificial mayfly against a natural has led to confusion over the years, and today there remains a strong division of opinion concerning what constitutes what.

I am able to recognise several species found on waters familiar to me, and I know of several others which I have yet to identify correctly. It is a complicated business, further compounded by variations from district to district. The problem besetting most anglers who become seriously involved is to know when to stop, for it can become a time-consuming business once a collection of specimens is begun. One begins with a collecting screen used for catching disturbed specimens from the stream bottom and later, when the duns and spinners are on the water, an angler has to decide whether he is an entomologist or a fisherman. It is an exasperating business attempting to catch a spinner in your hat when a fish is rising in the tail of the pool, and trying to mark down a dun as it lands in the bushes tends to be unrewarding.

A collection of specimens is however, rewarding in itself and adds to the enjoyment of a wonderful sport. But many successful anglers get by without ever knowing the scientific classification of the insect their quarry is feeding on, and even the scientists tell us that their knowledge of the order is very incomplete, so the angler is to be excused if his knowledge of this subject is not as wide as he would like. I put this business of matching the hatch to Robert K. Bragg of Christchurch, a professional fly-tier, who has lived in New Zealand since 1939 when he arrived from England fully trained in the craft after service with the well-known English tackle firm of Ogden Smiths. This is what he wrote:

Many years ago I used to enjoy browsing through a large cabinet in the Natural History Museum in South Kensington compiled by the entomologist Martin Mosley. Ephemeroptera (duns and spinners) were displayed in conjunction with artificial copies of the numerous insects in their stages of metamorphosis. The description tablet said: "This collection has been arranged not only to enable a fly fisherman to study the actual insects which his artificial patterns are intended to represent, but also to give some idea of the natural food of trout".

I believe that the New Zealand Ephemeroptera comprise approximately one-fifth of the insect orders upon which trout feed in this country. I believe that a project, such as Mosley's and on a reduced scale, due to the declining number of Ephemeroptera species still existing in New Zealand would not only encourage more interest in fly fishing (against chuck-and-chance-it) but that conservation would be fostered by presenting the specimens in light of modern scientific research.

For the angler Bragg recommends as follows: "Specimens should be collected from the nymph stage upwards and classified with the help of a qualified entomologist specialising in the order. Information sifted regarding the approximate artificial (not necessarily exact) imitation combined with the aid of a fly-tier doing his job to complete the project. Observant anglers fishing a stretch of water

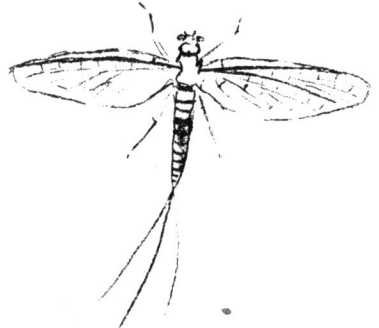

approximate wing span ⅞ in or 22 mm

ONE OF THE "RED SPINNERS"

As the name suggests the general tone of this insect is of a sepia colour. The wings are more fragile than any drawing could convey and have a faint sepia tone throughout the veining.

According to Phillips this fly is found in the later part of summer but the specimens in my collection were found in late October in Hawke's Bay.

Deleatidium nymph

Mayfly hovering

regularly become acquainted with periodic fly hatches and have, through experience, the right medicine in their fly boxes to cope with any situation. ("I often feel that ignorance is bliss)."

I think that Bragg has summed the situation up perfectly in his last two sentences. I have thought on occasions that the wide variation of public waters in this country have helped slow down the development of the higher art of dry fly fishing. In the United Kingdom we are told that practically all good waters are private and no doubt the anglers of that country are restricted in their choice of water. For the same reason they are very familiar with their own river or beat at all times of the season and must, if they are to enjoy their restrictions to the full, be in command of a very wide knowledge of the life habits of the insects they seek to copy in an endeavour to fool their quarry. In this country we bundle our gear into the car and have the choice of practically any stream or lake we wish to drive to. This diversification of allegiance is responsible for so many of us not having as complete a knowledge of a stream as could be wished, especially in relation to the Ephemeroptera that inhabit its pools and runs.

There are several flies of New Zealand origin that are intended as copies of the indigenous species, but many naturals are adequately catered for in the wide selection of duns and spinners that have for so long proved so successful in all parts of the temperate world where trout abound. In the section on dry and wet flies the reader will find them all listed. There is a type of dry fly fisherman who will attempt to match exactly the particular species of Ephemeroptera which trout are taking at the moment, while others have, through experience, found that a few simple dressings will give an adequate representation of all species. In support of the latter school is the fact that we are inclined to inspect the natural and artificial from a dorsal aspect, whereas the trout see their victims as a gauzy silhouette. And more important than all these considerations is the size of the artificial. Even two of the largest species of our mayflies (*Oniscigaster distans* and *Coloburiscus humeralis*) are approximated in size by a No. 14 hook (old scale) the rest of the species being more adequately matched by a No. 16 or even 18. Nos 10 and 12 may be all right for large beetle-type or sedge flies, but I doubt whether they have any place in a box of duns and spinners, especially if the water is clear and the trout wary.

FLIES (DIPTERA)

This term loosely covers the larger members of the Diptera group. The largest is the common black blowfly, the smallest the housefly, apart from odd smaller specimens that an angler will occasionally come across but never bother to identify. We must not forget the blue bottle and the brown bottle as well as the hover fly.

All of these creatures start off as maggots in rotting matter. In the back country the large black blowfly is common and breeds in damp rotting vegetable material. Any angler who has camped in the back country is well acquainted with the manner in which this pest descends in buzzing hordes whenever camp is set up.

Blowflies and other flies, while being terrestrial creatures, often end up in the water in great numbers. I have caught trout that were full of them and a large black type of fly is often well taken. A Black Gnat is the favourite of most, but there are other patterns that will also kill effectively. Several of the fat-bodied peacock herl patterns are probably taken as blowflies.

You will never get a rise to blowflies like that to the beetle species, but for the dry fly fisherman who is working his way carefully up a stream covering all the likely lies, an artificial fly designed to copy one of the blowfly family will usually serve him well.

Blowfly, family Muscidae.

FRESHWATER CRAYFISH (CRUSTACEA)

The freshwater crayfish abounds in most lakes and streams in this country and is a favourite quarry of the trout during its nocturnal prowlings, when the crustacean has left the protection of its lair under the stones or among the water weeds in its scavenging

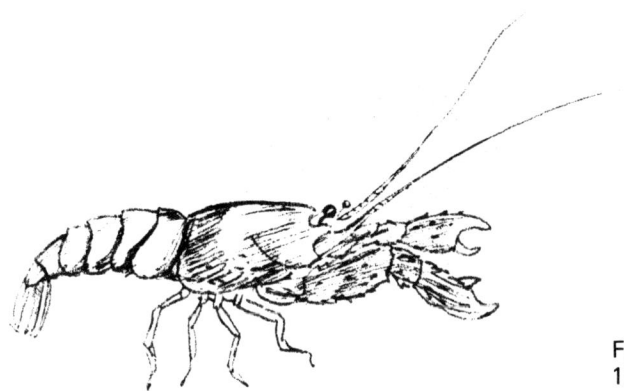

Freshwater crayfish, 1½ in to 6 in long.

searches across less protected areas of the water. There are three recorded species of freshwater crayfish in New Zealand, but for the purpose of the angler they are all classed as one. The effectiveness of some of the large type of lures is no doubt due to their being mistaken for a member of the crayfish family.

They range in length from the juvenile size of a fraction of an inch to some specimens six inches long. Many trout are caught with their stomachs hard and lumpy, filled with several crayfish. I have often caught fish with only a claw in their stomachs, their victims apparently having escaped with a mere amputation.

Some lures are claimed to be an exact representation of a crayfish. It cannot be denied that there is a superficial resemblance in the case of the Fuzzy Wuzzy, but where trout are prone to feed on these hard-shelled spiny creatures with menacing nippers, any big lure fished deep with a jerky retrieve will be well taken when the trout are in a responsive mood.

FRESHWATER SNAILS

In some lakes the freshwater snail may form a very important item of the trout's diet. I have seen lake trout with enlarged and distended vents due to their diet of snails, the shell of which did not dissolve or break down during digestion.

Often trout will be found with a stomach full of weed, but a closer inspection reveals that the weed is covered with small snails.

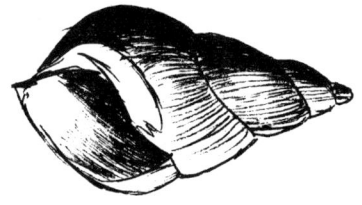

These small snails are of no consequence to the angler, but I have recorded an interesting and novel application of a fly fishing technique in attacking this problem. Mr Frank Lord's Snail Fly is dealt with elsewhere in the book.

ICHNEUMON FLIES (HYMENOPTERA)

There are several varieties of Ichneumon fly to be found near the water. Although of terrestrial origin, they are often found on the water, and consequently appear in autopsies of trout caught in summer. It is the opinion of some that the orange spinner is probably taken for an Ichneumon. They are a beautiful if rather venomous-looking insect and are readily identified by their slender waists and curled sicklelike abdomens. I have often wondered why someone hasn't deliberately dressed a fly around the bend of the hook to copy the curve of this insect's body.

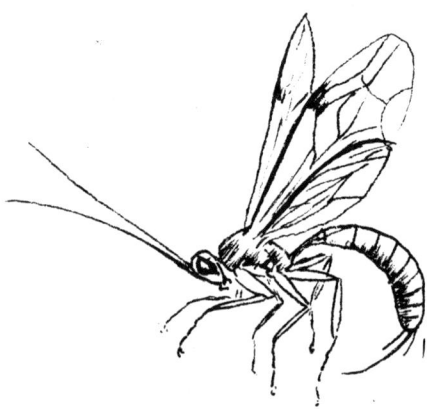

Ichneumon fly, 1 in long.

LACE-WINGS (NEUROPTERA)

The order of Neuroptera is of interest to the New Zealand angler as in some swift stony rivers its larvae forms an important part of a trout's diet. Every angler is aware of the creeper or toe-biter, a multi-legged creature nearly 1½ inches long at maturity. The fly is not often seen by reason of its retiring nature, but the female is a large insect with a wing span of three inches. The male is a little over half that size.

The trout fisherman has not exploited this insect to the full and I know of no artificial fly tied with the purpose of imitating it. I have dealt more fully with this under the section devoted to the Alder Fly.

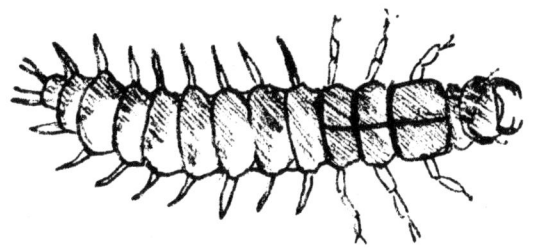

Toe biter, or creeper, *Archichauliodes diversus*, larva of the New Zealand alder fly.

MIDGES (DIPTERA)

The larvae of the midge, called the bloodworm, lives in streams that suffer from pollution, but there is one species that is to be found in many clear trout streams. This is the pale green worm that encases itself in a thin-walled case on silt-covered stones. I used to think that this worm was a member of the caddis family, but have since learnt that it is a midge larvae. The adult is a small sandflylike creature that swarms on the stream surface on a warm evening. All the small trout in the stream come up to feed on them, as do many of the smaller indigenous minnows.

There are several other species of midges to be found in and on the streams, but it has been my experience that they are all too small to be of consequence to the angler. We must not confuse these insects with the so-called "midge" of some Southland rivers, which are a small species of Ephemeroptera.

MINNOWS AND OTHER SMALL FISH

Some trout don't wait until they have reached large size before they start feeding on smaller fry. I have had fish just over legal taking size which have been full of smelt, whitebait or bullies.

Most of the streamlined style of lures are tied with the express purpose of imitating small fish and are retrieved with dash to help impart this impression to the larger fish below.

One of the most common small fishes is the whitebait, (*Galaxias attenuatus*). The immature fish enter the rivers from the seas in large shoals and the trout prey on them with abandon. A small slim fly fished across a trout busily engaged in slashing among whitebait in the shallows is usually well taken. There is another small fish, the smelt, to be found in the inland lakes as well as in the rivers. It looks superficially like the whitebait but it is of a different family altogether (Retropinna), there being several species. One of these is to be found entering the river at the same time as the whitebait, while another species is found landlocked in inland lakes. This last species has been planted in many waters where it did not previously exist, Taupo being one place where its introduction has resulted in phenomenal success. When they spawn along the shallow margins of the lakes in spring and summer they become easy prey for the trout and a special style of fishing, known as smelting, has evolved. It involves the use of a floating line and a slim sparsely-dressed fly fished quickly over an area where trout indicate their presence by the wild swirls and splashes that accompany their predatory forages. Perhaps the best type of fly to simulate these small fish is a Grey Ghost. A trayful of these flies looks almost exactly like a dish of whitebait or immature smelt.

Both the whitebait and smelt adults have a superficial similarity and they are both commonly referred to by the Maori name of *inanga*. The smelt may be identified by its cucumberlike smell, which once gave it the name of cucumber fish. Also, being related to the salmonoids, it possesses an adipose fin. Adults of both species rise freely to midges and can be easily mistaken for immature trout. I have often had them take a small fly in the evening.

Another important food fish is the cockabully (*Gobiomorphus* spp) a bottom-dwelling minnow that frequents the shallow margins of lakes and rivers. For many years it was the practice of anglers to use the "bully" for bait and countless tons of trout must have been taken over the years with this small fish. With a large flattened head and

Adult form of whitebait, *Galaxias attenuatus*.

Immature trout

Adult form of smelt *(Retropinna)*.

Cock-a-bully, *Gobiomorphus*, spp.

a tapered body many lures have been tied to represent it and it can be said of all of them that they have succeeded.

Elvers are another item of food that trout relish. I have seen a countless procession of them migrating up a Hawke's Bay river. They formed a dark wavering column about three or four feet across and from where I first noticed them they continued downstream for over half a mile until the bank ran into willows and I could no longer ascertain how much farther down the line travelled. There must have been billions of them.

When considering the small fish that have become natural prey to the trout we must not forget the young of the trout themselves. From the time the young alevins leave the egg in the stream-bed gravel they are subject to the depredations of their elders, and in many streams no small trout up to as much as seven or eight inches long is free from the prospect of providing a meal for one of his elders.

SHRIMPS

As well as the shrimps proper, we include in this group, the larger fresh-water prawn. From an angler's point of view these creatures are invariably all classed as shrimps. They favour the slower reaches of the rivers and the brackish water of estuaries and lakes. They live among the waterweeds, along the cress edges and in the roots of bank-dwelling cover. The red-root mats of the willow are a favourite haunt.

In some districts the shrimp is a legal bait and anglers boil them briefly in a tin. When they turn white a couple are impaled on a hook and fished on a pater noster type of rig.

A fly or lure fisherman's interest in these creatures is shown in several ways and I include dressings which are intended to imitate a shrimp. No doubt several other dressings could be taken for the animal if fished in the type of water they normally inhabit.

Fresh water prawn or shrimp, *Xiphocaris*. Body size 1 in.

STONE FLIES (PLECOPTERA)

This order of insects is of great importance to the angler. Some streams carry a very heavy stream-bed population of their larvae and in others, particularly the South Island, trout will be taken that have been feeding on them exclusively. The first stonefly larvae I found was taken on first sight to be an earwig of sorts. There are three species: the long-tailed (*Zelandoperla maculata*), the short-tailed (*Aucklandobius trivacuata*), and the green stonefly (*Stenoperla prasina*). The adults are to be found among the stones along the river's edge. They fly but little, and only at dusk and after dark. The first two are sombre-looking creatures about half an inch long, while the green stonefly, over an inch in length, is readily recognised. There are several artificial flies to copy both the adults and nymphs.

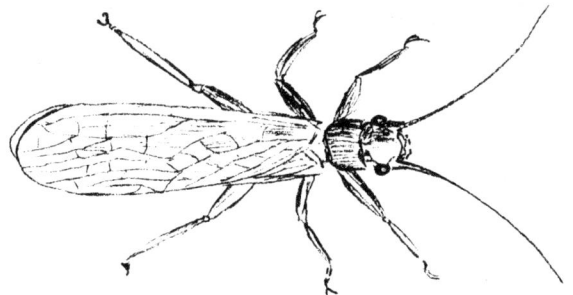

New Zealand stonefly, *Stenoperla prasina*.
Its actual size is 1⅛ in, not including antennae.

2

LURES

TAUPO AND ROTORUA

The flies or lures used in the Taupo-Rotorua districts are unique to New Zealand and now widely used over much of the country. In fact these streamer flies are now exported to other parts of the globe. In the early days salmon flies were used to catch the large rainbow trout which live a salmonlike existence in the North Island lakes. The first deviations from the ornate salmon flies closely followed the basic procedure of winging and body construction as laid down in the traditional dressing of these large flies. Turkey feather and mallard were substituted for the more exotic and brilliantly dyed mixed wing, and the bodies became less complicated, chenille or wool taking the place of colourful floss, herl and tinsel.

But for many years New Zealand tiers remained under the influence of the salmon fly to the extent that they still dressed their bodies with a silver tag, a tail of golden pheasant crest or tippet, and often a topping of golden pheasant. The last examples of this type of fly disappeared about thirty years ago. Today the fly of the old salmon mould has almost disappeared and rarely is an angler to be found using, say, a Turkey and Yellow with a long free wing. His fly will probably be tied in the manner of a split wing and made from grouse tail. Perhaps one of the most popular types of tie is the Parson's Glory style of streamer. This fly is closely allied to the American streamer fly, which is tied in much the same manner except that the long neck or saddle hackles "stream" free, and when cast with a fly rod the feathers have the annoying habit of wrapping around the shank of the hook and locking in the bend. To overcome this the Americans use a long shank hook with the bend close under the tail of the wing. The New Zealand custom is to use an ordinary Limerick hook and take the tinsel ribbing through the wing or streamer feathers. This helps overcome the wrapping problem. Just who introduced this method of tying a fly is hard to say, although Phil Parson's wonderful fly and James Ross's Taupo Tiger were probably among the first to be tied in this manner.

Another style of lure is the killer, brain child of Frank Lord of Rotorua. There is hardly an angler who hasn't heard of Lord's

Killer. Today there are several killers to be found in the tackle shops as well as a legion of home-tied favourites.

The first of the pukeko flies was Craig's Nighttime, the creation of E. (Scotty) Craig of Auckland. The popularity of this type of dressing has been borne out by the many variations on the original theme.

The smelt fly can be any pattern slimly dressed on a small hook, and fished with the dart and dash of these small fish which form so much a part of the diet of our trout from Rotorua to the sea-run trout of Southland.

There has been a great proliferation of lures in the last decade. Many shops have their own specials and commercial interests dream up new patterns to catch anglers. No doubt those worthy of serious consideration will survive. Others, like fashions, will be forgotten.

CANTERBURY LURES

Many patterns were devised on Lake Ellesmere and the Selwyn mouth, and today some of these lures are used over the whole of the country. Perhaps some of the best known of these are the Hope's series, which were the design of Mr Dave Hope of Christchurch.

These flies replaced the large salmon and sea trout flies that were once used, and the natural bully, also once a popular bait along with the soleskin and devon minnows, soon lost favour to the new feather lures. In my experience the Canterbury lures have been heavier and chunkier than the Taupo and Rotorua flies. The feathers of hens or the wide spade hackles of cocks tend to be used rather than the neck hackles used so much in the northern patterns.

In addition to Dave Hope, some of the anglers directly involved in the development of these patterns were R. K. Bragg, R. L. Brunton, R. Christie, G. Everett, W. Winchester, and W. Wooster.

As elsewhere many patterns were dropped as improved patterns took their place. Many North Island anglers have benefitted, and of course the reverse applies equally as well.

The originality of some flies is in question. There can be no doubt that there are few dressings or variations that haven't already been tried at some time or other. Heaven knows how many fly-tiers have dreamed up their own patterns, innocently unaware that the same principle has been tried before. In a recent case an angler claimed in a publication to have invented a fly that was in use forty years ago.

I myself have come across this sort of thing several times, and in at least one case I made myself very unpopular by pointing out that a certain fly one angler was claiming as his own invention was in fact an old English fly that had been around for ages. I did not doubt the sincerity of the person concerned, it was just a case of the pattern being developed in all innocence. As anglers proliferate and more of them begin tying their own flies, no doubt the same sort of thing will happen again. Recently in an American magazine a great write-up was given to a couple of anglers who had developed a "no hackle" dry fly, the fly riding on the whisks of fur protruding from a rough dubbing body. If the two anglers concerned had been students of angling history they would have discovered that the English had long before developed the Hare's Ear, which is tied in its proper form with no hackle and floats on its untidy thorax of spiky hare's fur.

In some cases the double naming of flies has arisen as a result of commercial interests marketing a fly under their own name rather than using the original name given by its creator or the firm that first put the pattern on the market. It is fair to comment that many of these situations have occurred through jealousy and even spite. Occasionally when tracking down a confused pattern I have found that the last ravels of the skein led to an early dispute between rival commercial interests.

ALL BLACK   HOOK: 2–8
Body, wing and hackle:
All tied of black materials with a silver rib.
This pattern was no doubt inspired by our famous Rugby Football team. Who tied the first fly remains a mystery, but I have come across it in several catalogues. It is a night fly.

AWAHOU

See Leslie's Lure. The name Awahou was given to the Leslie by a tackle firm in opposition to the one that first introduced the pattern commercially.

BADGER   HOOK: 2–8
Body: White chenille
Wing: Badger hackle
Hackle: Badger hackle

This lure is fairly well known in the South Island. In the north it would have its head painted red and be called a white Taupo Tiger. Either way, it is basically the same pattern. There can be no doubt the Badger evolved separately from the Tiger.

BARRED ROCK LURES   HOOK: 2–8

BARRED ROCK WHITE:
Body: White
Wing and Hackle: Barred Rock
BARRED ROCK SILVER:
Body: Silver
Wing and Hackle: Barred Rock
Wing overlay: Grey mallard
BARRED ROCK RED:
Body: Red
Wing and Hackle: Barred Rock

This range of lures is associated with Mr W. (Bill) Winchester of Leeston and while they would probably be classed as "Dorothys" by North Island anglers, these Canterbury lures were originally tied using soft hen and spade hackles, being shorter and chunkier than the Taupo Dorothys.

BISHOP'S BLESSING   HOOK: 2–8   KILWELL
Wing feather: Honey grizzle
Body: Flat silver tinsel
Rib: Oval tinsel
Tag: Red
Hackle: Honey grizzle

This fly is very popular as a harling pattern and it kills well as a stream fly. Most anglers prefer it to be tied with pale feathers. It was designed by Kilwell of Rotorua. As John Wells told me: "We had a Parson's Glory, a Pope's Nondescript, a Silver Priest, so why not a Bishop's Blessing?"

You will sometimes hear this pattern called a "Silver Parsons".

Lures

BLACK PHANTOM HOOK: 2–8 KILWELL
Wing or Side Wings: Black feathers from back and rump of pukeko
Tail: Black squirrel
Body: Black with silver tinsel rib
Cheek: Jungle cock

An excellent lure for night fishing, it is tied in two ways. The feathers are either placed or top of the hook as with most pukeko flies, or tied on the side of the body, two or three to each side. Jungle cock feathers are more neatly and easily tied using the second method. In the absence of jungle cock, which is becoming harder to procure, the white-centred flank feathers of a Californian quail make a passable substitute.

BLACK PRINCE HOOK: 2–8
Wing feathers: Black cock hackles
Body: Black chenille or wool, with silver ribbing
Tag: Red
Hackle: Black

A good night fly which probably originated in the Rotorua district. However, there is a fly used in the South Island called the Hart Creek which is dressed in an identical manner. Its correct name depends on where you come from.

BLONDIE HOOK: 4–8
Wing: Blonde hair, preferably that of a child, which is softer and flows better in the water
Body: Silver with a few whisks of dyed red hackle

This fly is a great killer when the trout are chasing whitebait in the shallows of a river or lake. It does have a problem, however: If tied too long the hair is inclined to wrap around the shank during casting. The best way to overcome this is to shorten the hair — and if you make your own flies you should procure some long shanked hooks. There have been many variations of the Blondie. I have seen pale floss used, although it soon matted and lost its effectiveness. Today a popular commercial substitute is the synthetic fibre used for making dolls' hair. When I was a youngster I used to tic a very effective Blondie from the pale hair in the tail of the jersey house cow's heifer calf. Copper wire dipped in vinegar and lacquered to retain its brightness was used for the body.

BLUE MALLARD   HOOK: 6–10
Tail: Mallard flank dyed blue
Body: Silver
Wing: Strip of mallard flank dyed blue

This pattern is a smelt fly, effectively fished fast on a floating line and cast among smelting trout.

BROWN KILLER   HOOK: 4–8
Tail: Brown squirrel
Body: Yellow wool
Side feathers: The dark chestnut-brown breast feathers of a shoveller drake

This fly is one of my own inventions and it is a great little lure. It will never become a commercial proposition as the plumage is not easily obtained.

While the shoveller, or spoonbill duck, is still found in some areas in reasonable numbers, in most districts its population is rather sparse. The breast of the female is also of a reddish-brown hue, but not with the same intensity as the drake.

BROWN QUAIL LURE

Anyone who does much shooting will surely have come across the little brown quail. Don't throw its feathers away. You will find that the flank feathers make excellent killer-type lures. With a squirrel tail and body colour to suit you can tie up a fly similar in colouring and marking to a Lord's Killer.

BRUNTON No. 1   HOOK: 2–6   L. BRUNTON
Tail: Brown. Hackle bunched
Body: White floss ribbed with silver
Wing: Wide brown hackles
Cheeks: Speckled Paradise breast feathers
Hackle: Brown

Lures

BRUNTON No. 2   HOOK: 2–6   L. BRUNTON
Tail: Ginger, hackle bunched
Body: White floss ribbed silver
Wing: Ginger hackles
Topping: Green Peacock sword
Hackle: Ginger

BRUNTON RED   Hook: 2–6   L. BRUNTON
Tail: Furnace hackle bunched
Body: Red with silver ribbing
Wing: Red furnace
Topping: Green peacock sword
Hackle: Red cock

These patterns were Canterbury favourites twenty years ago and were designed by Lou Brunton, a Christchurch angler, for use at the Selwyn mouth at Lake Ellesmere.

BUCKTAILS

This is an American term for a fly made from the tail hairs of a whitetail buck. All of these flies are streamers, to use another American term, and there can be no doubt that they are extremely effective. The term has now been broadened so that a bucktail may be tied from several other types of hair or a mixture such as polar bear, calf or kip, eland, or squirrel — you name it and it's probably been tried. I have used this type of fly for several years now, adding the appropriately coloured hair to tie bucktail versions of old New Zealand favourites such as the Taupo Tiger, Parson's Glory and Ewe Wasp, to name but a few. I would not suggest that these flies are better than the standard type of lure but I am sure they are equally as good. I mention this because the materials used are all obtainable in New Zealand as home-grown products, and as many of the imported materials used in fly-tying are of Asiatic origin, there is no guarantee that supplies will always be available.

BUGS BUNNY   HOOK: 2–8   W. WILLIS
This fly was originated by Mr Walter Willis of Te Kuiti, who called it the Willis Rabbit. However, the pattern is now tied by

Kilwell under the above name. It is a brute of a thing to tie as it takes time, and uses up twice as much skin as an ordinary rabbit fly, as well as a tail of squirrel fur which becomes more expensive every year. In fact this pattern is really one for the home tier. The tail of barred squirrel is tied in as normal. Then a strip of rabbit skin is cut across the pelt. One end is tied in at the tail and then wound up the body with the fur lying back, each succeeding turn overlaying the previous one. Once the top is reached a nice grizzle hackle can be added if required. Though I don't care to tie this fly myself I must admit that it pulses beautifully in the water. These are great lures to use on migratory fish. Illustrated is a nice specimen in black tied by its creator, complete with an eye painted on the head. The soft black fur came from a wild cat.

BULLY LURE

This is a term often loosely applied to any fly that resembles a cockabully and is fished in short slow jerks above the bottom of the lake or stream. The term usually describes the type of lure, rather than denoting a specific dressing. R. K. Bragg ties lures called Yellow and Red Bullys.

BULLY (RED and YELLOW)   HOOK: 4–8   R. K. BRAGG

These lures were designed by R. K. Bragg and are very similar in appearance to the Hamill's Killer, a pattern that has superseded them. Except for the golden pheasant tippets over the tail of the former, there is little difference.

BUM FLY   HOOK: 4–8

Body: Cheviot wool dyed to suit, usually green, yellow, orange or red

Tail and Wings: Chestnut-coloured rump feathers of a cock pheasant

The tail and two bunches of wing are tied in progressively, building the body as they go. The fly was originated in a Gisborne tackle shop and apparently after inspecting it someone remarked that it was a "bum-looking sort of fly".

I have it from several sources that it is a good fly and I've been asked to copy it for anglers. I didn't know the name until John Cockburn came along with a sample to be tied for an angler he knew. He was able to give me the story of its beginnings. Cheviot wool, which is very fine and crimpy, is ideal for this type of body. It spins on to the thread well, still retaining that slightly scraggy look which the fly's supporters insist must be part of its character.

CAPTAIN MILNE   HOOK: 2–6   D. HOPE
Body: Black with silver ribbing
Wing: 2 large paradise duck speckled feathers tied in at the head and secured at the butt with several turns of black thread. In this manner the feathers form both wings and tail
Hackle: Black

This fly is a good night pattern and like the other Canterbury lures was designed for use at the Selwyn mouth. I have used a pattern of this type with success at Taupo.

CARDINAL   HOOK: 2–8
Body: Red wool or chenille, ribbed with silver tinsel
Wing and hackle: Cock dyed cardinal red

This is an old Taupo fly which was used a long time ago but has never really taken on. But like all trout flies it will of course take trout provided it is used at the right time in the right place. It is regarded as a night fly.

CHRISTIE   HOOK: 2–8   R. CHRISTIE
Body: Red
Wing: Ginger
Hackle: Black

This is another Canterbury lure. At the period they were being developed, the Christie was highly thought of, and some anglers still use the pattern.

COACHMAN LURE HOOK: 2–8
Tail: Tippets
Body: Bronze peacock herl
Wing: White swan, tied long
Hackle: Red cock

I have in my possession some old flies used by the late Mr W. Branson, an old angler who fished Taupo for years. He had several Coachmen in his box, tied long and slim with a long swept-back wing of white swan. It is a very streamlined-looking fly and without any doubt would kill fish. An angler of Branson's reputation would never have had them in his box if they weren't effective.

Another successful version of the Coachman is the Bucktail. I have used this pattern myself and it will take trout as efficiently as most flies. The pattern used was livened by the addition of a red tag.

CRAIG'S NIGHT-TIME HOOK: 2–10 E. CRAIG
Body: Black wool or chenille, ribbed with silver tinsel
Wing: Blue pukeko breast feathers
Tag: Red
Hackle: Black
Topping: One jungle cock eye laid on top of the blue wings

This fly is widely recognised as the first to incorporate pukeko feathers in its make-up. Its creator, Mr Eric Craig of Auckland, made it up nearly forty years ago. He picked up the feathers while walking along the banks of the Waitahanui Stream and heading back to the lodge he tied them into a fly. That night out in the rip he made a killing while most of the other anglers met with no luck. Fred Fletcher, the lodge proprietor, asked to see the fly and sent the recipe away to one of the commercial fly-tiers. It has been at the top of the sales list ever since. Tied small on a No. 10 it is a good stream or river fly for night fishing and I have found that it kills well if fished on a floating line along the edge of a gentle current. Tied on large hooks it is fished deep and if the bottom permits, slowly.

DAPPLED DOG HOOK: 4–8 G. SANDERSON
Tail: Grey barred squirrel
Body: Fluorescent chenille (lime green or orange)
Hackles: Two grizzle hackles, one wound in half way along body.

This pattern of Sanderson's is an excellent lure for lake run rainbows. It was first used with success on the Tongariro but will take trout well everywhere. For a couple of winters several years ago I used hardly any other fly. In the winter of 1960 I took 153 trout in three months, most of them on this dressing. It is an excellent teaser to use on fresh-run fish and I have found that an orange dappled dog will on occasions entice the dourest of fish if it is shown to them for long enough. I have had some success with the green version in the smaller sizes and remember a bag of twelve fish it took for me in the Waikato one early morning. The dappled dog is not as well known as it should be. I have also seen this pattern sold under the name of Grey Fuzzy Wuzzy. Geoff Sanderson insists that the fly should be dressed with a fluorescent body.

DEMON (GOLD OR SILVER)   HOOK: 2–8
Wing: Bronze mallard flank
Body: Flat tinsel, gold or silver
Hackle: Orange, also whisks
Cheeks: Jungle cock

The Demon is an old English sea-trout pattern, often tied as a salmon fly. It was a very popular rainbow pattern years ago and there is still a demand for it. It is a lovely-looking fly and there can hardly be an angler who hasn't been tempted at some time or other and come out of the tackle shop with one or two, even if for no other reason than that they look very dashing in a flybox, especially if they're cheeked with jungle cock. The Demon is a good bright day fly and if you have ever beached a fine fresh-run rainbow with a Demon glittering in the corner of his jaw you will admit it makes a fine sight. The dressing described above will be found in most of the tackle shops, although it differs in some respects from the old-world pattern, which itself has several variations.

DEMON SQUIRREL   HOOK: 2–8
Tail. Golden pheasant topping
Body: Flat gold tinsel
Wing: Brown squirrel tail
Hackle: Orange

This is a Demon with a brown hair wing and is a lure that R. K. Bragg esteems on the southern scene. This pattern is also a good Taupo river pattern.

DEVIL DODGER   HOOK: 2–8
Body: Silver
Wing: Black
Hackle: Black

This fly is dressed in a slimmer manner than the conventional Canterbury lures. It is usually regarded as a night fly but will on occasions take well during daylight hours.

DOROTHY   HOOK: 2–8
Body: Wool or chenille, usually yellow or red although all the popular colours can be used. The silver body is another favourite
Wing and Hackle: Well-barred grizzle

The Dorothy is a good traditional fly although not so much in favour as it was some years ago. But as a pattern it has its devotees and for them it kills as well as any other pattern. Personally I have never considered it too highly as a bright day fly, preferring the Parsons or the Tiger. However, in the evening or during a change of light, I think it is a very hard fly to beat, particularly if it has a red body.

DUCHESS   HOOK: 2–8   KILWELL
Body: Yellow with silver rib
Side feathers: The golden black-tipped feathers from a cock pheasant's flank, tied in two a side.
Tail: A bunch of fibres from a cock pheasant tail

This is a pattern that has never really taken on and there is only a limited demand for the dressing. It is, however, a good Taupo fly and I know of some good bags taken on it.

EWE WASP (OR TAUPO WASP)   HOOK: 2–8

There are several stories relating to the origin of this fly. To me the most plausible one is that it was an early derivation of the Jock Scott, a fine old salmon fly very much in vogue years ago. The fly has the colour "balance" of a Jock Scott, and the Ewe Wasp tied forty years ago is a very different tie from that found today.

John Wells thought that the original was an obscure English pattern, but he would not be too sure on this point. Fred Fletcher used to claim that there was an insect found in the Taupo area called the ewe wasp, although one of his contemporaries, G. G. Kelly, claimed that he had never come across the "ram wasp" yet. Fred Fletcher claimed that the ewe wasp was common in the region of the Roto-ngaio lagoon, and when about, was well taken by the trout.

With due respect to the opinion of an old friend, I suspect that there is more to it than that. I myself have not been able to track down any such insect, so the name is probably a local one. However, I have noticed in the district that there are times when the little native burrowing bee hovers in its thousands among the flowers of the native shrubs. This insect has a yellow and blackish body and therein might lie the clue. But again, to suggest that a ewe wasp fly tied on a No. 2 or even 1/0 represents a small insect is stretching the imagination too far. Let's start off with the early pattern.

Body: In two parts, of wool or floss. Front black, rear portion pale yellow

Ribbing: Oval silver tinsel

Wing: Bronze mallard flank. This was usually bolstered with an inside wing of turkey

Hackle: Black

Tag: Silver tinsel

Tail: Golden pheasant crest

Cheeks: Jungle cock

By today's standards that is a fancy sort of fly. I have even seen it tied with a butt of black herl and golden pheasant topping as well. But as the years went by, materials became dearer and labour cost more, so the little fancy bits were omitted. Bronze mallard became too expensive and the turkey that had hidden beneath became the accepted thing. Anglers liked plumper bodies, so chenille replaced the floss. The fish didn't seem to notice when the Golden Pheasant luxuries dropped off, and today most anglers complain even about the price of jungle cock cheeks!

The Ewe Wasp has killed countless trout over the years, mostly at night. It is a fly favoured by some anglers on a semi-moonlit night. They feel that as it is a mixture of black and yellow it has something to offer no matter if the moon is shining or obscured by cloud. When they catch fish on it who can dispute them.

FERRIS (RED and YELLOW)
Body: Red or yellow wool or chenille
Wing feathers: Two white hackles inside two black hackles
Hackle: Black
Ribbing: Silver

I once used this fly quite a lot. It was effective on the Hawke's Bay rivers and one morning at the Waitahanui rip I had great sport. It was one of those times when I caught fish and no one else had a pull. I think that if you went into most tackle shops today you would be lucky to find a Ferris in their trays, which is a pity. John Wells of Rotorua tells me that the first Ferris was tied by his firm of Kilwells for an English angler by the name of Ferris. Apparently the first pattern was tied from the soft thigh feathers of a buff bantam. How the transition to the patterns given above came about is not known.

FUZZY WUZZY   HOOK: 2–8   FRED FLETCHER
Body: Red or black chenille or wool. Other colours are also used, the green and orange both having their adherents
Tail: Black squirrel
Hackles: Two black hackles tied in one at the head, the other halfway along the body. On a small fly, one hackle at the head is used, on an extra large fly, three hackles.

This pattern used to be called Fletcher's Fuzzy Wuzzy when it was first tied in the 1930s. It was the brainchild of the late Fred Fletcher, "Mr Hundred Per Cent" who built and ran the Waitahanui Lodge. This fly is referred to by many anglers as a Hairy Dog, but this is not correct. Fred told me that he tied the fly with the idea of simulating a freshwater crayfish, and he used a large hackle wound palmerwise along the body to represent the legs of the *koura*. When retrieved in short jerks the legs would draw in against the body then spread out again as the fly paused. That was Fred's idea and the fly became, and still is, one of the most hard to beat, and even during the day can be a very effective fly. The tie has been streamlined with the years, but this hasn't detracted from the lure's efficiency.

FLUORESCENT FLIES

This is a general term describing the type of body material used rather than signifying a pattern. It began after the war with the introduction of gatron yarn and later other materials dyed with fluorescent dies began to appear. We are all now aware of these colours, whether we fish or not, as they are used on advertising signs, warning signals etc. Their application to fly tying has been a success, but like many others I am not wholly convinced. Proponents of the materials claim that they are highly attractive to trout in the early morning and dusk, especially when the river is carrying a little colour. Now we all know that dawn and dusk are the most effective times to fish anyway, so that a trout which took a fly with a fluorescent body would probably have been equally receptive to a regular pattern. I cannot say what the story is with coloured water, not having used them much under those conditions.

But there is a growing number of anglers who insist that their flies be tied with this type of body, and the most popular colour is a bright lime green. Certainly there are times, particularly with migratory rainbows, when the fish seem to show a preference for this type of fly. To a cagey brown taking his breakfast in his own pool they might appear outlandish, but to a sulking rainbow lying within the strange confines of a river pool after a lifetime of wide open water, the bright colour might mean the difference between complete indifference and an ill-humoured snap.

FURRY BUTCHER   HOOK: 2–8   KILWELL
Body: Silver
Tail: Squirrel
Wing: Squirrel
Hackle: Orange

Here is a fly that appeals to me. It has everything a good stream fly should have, slimness with a dash of brightness and colour. It is a Rotorua fly, but will kill well anywhere where the trout are prone to helping themselves to whitebait or smelt. The fly should not be overdressed and the fur-wing kept a bit on the short side so that it doesn't foul the bend of the hook.

GINGER MICK   HOOK: 2–8   KILWELL
Body: Chenille or wool. Yellow, red or green. Silver rib
Wing: Ginger cock
Hackle: Ginger

This fly is closely related to the Parson's Glory, and I have seen versions of both that could have passed one for the other. To be classed as a true Ginger Mick though, the feather should be as the name implies. Some trollers use this fly to the exclusion of all others, but it would be true to say that the majority of fishermen find the paler Parson's has the edge over it in the long run.

GINGER SMELT
Tail: Golden pheasant tippets
Body: White with silver rib
Wing: Ginger hackles trailing free and not secured along body with rib.

This pattern, excellent for harling, is a curse to fly-cast, as the trailing feathers so often wrap around the bend of the hook.

GOLDEN LION   HOOK: 2–6   R. K. BRAGG
Tail: Golden pheasant topping
Body: Flat gold with red seal's fur at shoulder
Wing: Black tied down with gold oval
Hackle: Gallina
Topping: Peacock sword

Derived from one of Ogden Smiths of London's patterns and introduced and styled for New Zealand fishing by the Christchurch fly-tier R. K. Bragg.

GREEN DRAGON   R. K. BRAGG
Body: Green
Wing: Black with green overlay
Hackle: Black
Rib: Silver

This fly is sometimes confused with the Green Orbit and I have often seen the latter called a Green Dragon. However, as the above dressing indicates there is a fair difference between these two flies.

Lures

GREY GHOST   HOOK: 2–10   KILWELL
Body: Silver, with silver rib
Wing: Cock hackle dyed grey
Hackle: Grey

    Like all good flies the Grey Ghost is simplicity itself. If you have ever seen a saucer full of these flies as they come off the vice you could be tempted to make them into whitebait fritters. If a home tier paints the heads grey and adds a small white eye with a black centre the likeness is even greater. There can be no doubt that the Ghost's most effective patterns are those tied on small hooks, 8's or even 10's. As with other flies the Ghost, due to popular demand, is also turned out with different coloured bodies, the most popular being the green, especially the fluorescent green which is rapidly becoming a very popular fly in the Taupo district. The home tier is well advised to drop the hackle from his fly. It isn't the least bit necessary and can give a lumpy head if not tied in correctly. The Ghost is a very effective fly for smelting fish and can also be used as a harling fly. The version with the fluorescent body is very effective on trout which have just arrived in the river from the lake.

GREEN SLEEVES   HOOK: 4–8   R. K. BRAGG
Tail: Black squirrel
Body: Green wool
Side feathers: Grey partridge dyed green

    This is a Canterbury pattern that closely resembles a Green Hamill's Killer.

GUARDSMAN   HOOK: 2–8
Tail: Black squirrel
Body: Black chenille with silver rib
Wing: Red breast feathers of a golden pheasant
Hackle: Black

    This is a night lure of my own design. It is an attractive-looking pattern and has proved itself on many occasions.

HAIR FLIES

The hair fly is excellent for use on rainbow trout and sea-run browns. The only real commercial version is the Blondie, which is normally tied from human hair with a body of silver tinsel. Some shop versions are now tied with artificial hair of the synthetic material used in making dolls' wigs. Hamill's Silver Smelt, using a mixture of green and white fibre, is a tie very much favoured by some anglers.

As a youngster I used to tie a hair fly from the tail hair of a Jersey heifer, and these did very well in Hawke's Bay, where a hair fly has always been in favour. There is no set tie, as apart from the two commercial patterns mentioned above, most are home-tied. It is an easy pattern to make up so long as too many turns aren't made round the head, and the hair is well glued in with lacquer. A trout smashing around in the shallows of the river is usually responsive to a hair fly fished through his patrol. They are best tied in the smaller sizes and the hair should be tied in sparsely, in preference to a thick hank.

HAIRY DOG   HOOK: 2–8
Body: Wool or fur, black or red
Tail: Spaniel or squirrel fur
Wing: As above
Ribbing: Silver

As Joe Frost once wrote: . . . "And then they started making flies from the smelly parts of dogs".

Well I'm not sure about the smelly part, but the Hairy Dog's origin is related in Mr O. S. Hintz's fine book *Trout at Taupo*. Some wags staying at a Taupo Lodge tied the first fly from a black spaniel. Today the fly is tied from squirrel hair, but somehow or other the name Hairy Dog has attached itself to the Fuzzy Wuzzy, and this sometimes leads to confusion. I am pleased though to see that the tackle firms don't pander to popular opinion and change the names.

Lures

HALL'S NIGHTTIME HOOK: 4–8 D. HALL
Body: Red and black chenille twisted and wound along hook, giving a harlequin effect
Wing and Tail: Grizzle cock dyed red. No hackle. The wing feathers are tied in short and are not ribbed down with tinsel in the normal New Zealand manner

Eddie Bosomworth of Rotorua introduced me to this fly, which is the brainchild of Rotorua angler Dave Hall. Although well-known in the Geyserland area it has not yet extended elsewhere. But it enjoys a good reputation with those anglers who fish the mouths of Rotorua streams.

HAMILL'S KILLER HOOK: 4–8 W. HAMILL
Tail: Black squirrel tail
Body: Wool, red, green or yellow
Side feathers: Grey partridge dyed green tied in killer fashion

The Hamill's Killer is an excellent fly and while it is probably intended to imitate a bully there is strong evidence that in some lakes it is taken as a dragon fly nymph. The body of this fly is usually tied in red or yellow, the red being favoured for night fishing and the yellow during the day. The fly is the creation of Mr Bill Hamill of Rotorua.

HAMILL'S SMELT HOOK: 2–8
Body: Grey chenille
Wing: Two pale ginger hackles laid over two grizzle hackles. These are capped at the head with a v-cut from the grey breast plumage of a mallard drake

This fly comes from Mr Bill Hamill of Rotorua. While it is not a greatly-favoured pattern it is nevertheless a good fish-catcher. I have seen this pattern tied with a pale yellow body and used for harling with quite spectacular success.

HART'S CREEK   HOOK: 2-8
Tag: Red ibis (or dyed swan)
Body: Black with silver rib
Wing: Black
Hackle: Black

This fly, which R. K. Bragg tells me was the invention of Chamberlain of "Chamberlain's Ford", is almost identical to the Black Prince. It is normally tied in the manner of the Canterbury lure with heavy hackles and the wing tied in short. It is an excellent night fly.

HATEPE SMELT

These flies are difficult to describe except to say they are just a curl of natural sheep's wool loosely bound to a hook. They are drift-fished on a floating line along the edge of the rip, and unorthodox though they may seem they are apparently very deadly on occasions. John Cockburn of Hinemaiaia ties them from Romney wool and I know of several reputable anglers who think very highly of them. They were designed by Mr C. Rolleston.

HAWK

Body: Colour to suit with a preference for yellow or orange
Wing: Flank feathers of a harrier hawk tied in as a matuku
Ribbing: Oval tinsel

Twenty years ago the Hawk was a popular fly, although you will find it in few shops today. This is surprising, as it is a good killer when the trout are receptive. It is tied from the flank feathers of a harrier hawk and the paler the bird the better the fly. Young birds tend to have darker feathers of a brown hue whereas an old bird's feathers become a pale buff. Most hawks you see are youngsters and a few years ago when the Hawk fly was in vogue a certain tackle firm used to pay up to $4 for a good skin. However, with the demise of the rabbit the hawk population has suffered, and good skins are even harder to come by.

HAWK AND RABBIT

Body: White or green wool. These seem to be the most favoured colours for the fly although it is also tied in others

Tail: A pale strip cut from the primary feather of a harrier hawk wing

Shoulder: A small strip or bunch of rabbit fur. Some tie this with a strip of skin about half the length of the body, while others prefer a pinch of fur bunched on the shoulder and tied in at the head

This is a Rotorua fly and is used as a smelting pattern. It is popular, although I have always felt that there are other flies which do a better job of imitating a smelt. But some anglers swear by it, and that's as good a recommendation as anyone could wish for.

HILDA   HOOK: 2–6   W. WILLIS

Body: Wool. Yellow, red or green with flat silver ribbing
Wing: A bunch of fibres from the tail of a cock pheasant
Hackle: Nil
Eye: Yellow eyes are painted on the head by its creator

This fly was named by Willis after Mrs Hilda Smallman of Turangi. It is principally a harling pattern. Mrs Smallman was one of the first to use it, being so successful that she caught a trout large enough to win her a local angling club trophy. When tying this fly great care has to be exercised in having the bend of the fibres all lying the same way, or else it looks like a tattered shaving brush. The eye gives it a good minnow appearance.

HOPE'S SERIES

HOPE'S SILVERY   HOOK: 2–8   D. HOPE

Tail: Tip of barred rock feather
Body: White with flat silver ribbing
Wing: Pale buff or palest honey grizzle
Topping: Green peacock sword with a strip of pale blue floss silk laid along each side and caught under the ribbing

This is the best known of all the Canterbury lures and was intended to incorporate some of the outward aspects of the smelt or "Silvery", as it is known in some districts. The strip of floss is intended to impart the blueish tinge along the small fish's side.

Hope, who was one of the best-known anglers on the Christchurch scene, evolved this fly for use on Lake Ellesmere at the Selwyn mouth. It is a beautiful pattern which I personally prefer dressed in a streamlined manner. It is primarily a day fly but is considered by many to be good on a moonlight night.

HOPE'S RED-SILVERY   HOOK: 2–8   D. HOPE

Dressing the same as above, except that a red body is used.

HOPE'S DARK   HOOK: 2–8   D. HOPE
Tail: Tip of barred rock feather
Body: White with flat silver ribbing
Wing: Black hackles
Topping: Green peacock sword

JACK'S SPRAT   HOOK: 2–8   JACK ENGLAND
Body: Silver
Wing feather: Badger hackles
Hackle: Badger
Ribbing: Silver

Here is a good smelting fly, especially when tied in the smaller sizes. It has all the features a good smelt fly needs and if tied with jungle cock is very handsome. It was designed by Mr Jack England who ran a tackle business at Turangi on the Tongariro River.

Lures

JOCK MILLER   HOOK: 2–8
Tail: Two short points of grizzle hackle
Body: Wool (yellow, orange or red)
Wings: Several short tufts of rabbit fur tied in along the top of the body giving a continuous back of fur

This pattern is unusual and while not well-known, is an excellent lure for lake-run trout, especially with an orange body. The pattern shown was tied by John Cockburn of Hinemaiaia, who ties all his fur flies in this manner.

JUNGLE COCK

The "eye"-feather of jungle cock, used to dress so many lures and flies, is now on the way out owing to protection given to the bird in its Asian country of origin.

It would appear that jungle cock, especially on night flies, definitely improves the lure's effectiveness. I once used to doubt this but experience has shown me that flies with jungle cock eyes certainly catch more trout.

KEELER   HOOK: 2–8   KILWELL (WARWICK WELLS)
Tail: Brown squirrel tail
Body: Two sections, the rear yellow mohair, the front red wool
Wings: Back top, yellow golden pheasant rump feathers. Front top, red golden pheasant breast

It is no coincidence that this fly came on to the market at the time of a national political scandal in Britain. It is a pretty fly (as it should be) but while it is quite a successful lure I have found that it is more favoured in the extra large sizes and used for harling.

KILWELL No. 1   HOOK: 2–8
Tail: Black squirrel
Body: Wool. Yellow or red
Side feathers: Striped brown partridge

Many old anglers claim that this pattern is the old Mrs. Simpson and you will still find it under that label in some shops. It is now generally accepted, however as a Kilwell No. 1. Call it what you like, it is still a very good lure of the killer type, but it is doomed to pass from the scene as the supply of partridge plumage continues to dwindle.

KILWELL No. 2 HOOK: 2–8
Tail: Black squirrel
Body: Wool. Yellow or red
Side feathers: Mottled grouse plumage

Another killer pattern, this lure is not as well known as its stablemate. However, I am told it is an excellent night fly. There is no reason why it shouldn't be, as it has all the ingredients of a successful lure.

KIWI FLIES
Flies tied from the feathers of the kiwi were once highly regarded in the Taupo and Rotorua areas. They were tied in much the same manner as a Parson's Glory but their use has been banned to protect the bird.

LESLIE'S LURE LESLIE NEWDICK
Body: Yellow or red wool
Tail: A bunch of fibres from the tail feather of a cock pheasant.
Body feathers: Hen pheasant breast feathers or the small coverts from a hen pheasant wing, tied two a side.

This fly was the creation of Leslie Newdick, for many years the proprietor of the Spa Hotel, Taupo. While not as popular as it once was it is nevertheless a good fly of the bully type. This fly is sometimes referred to as an Awahou, but there can be no doubt that Newdick has first claim to this dressing.

LES'S FANCY HOOK: 2–8 L. HASTINGS
Wing: Strip of white rabbit
Body: White wool
Ribbing: Silver
Tag: Red wool
Head: Red

I have many times come across variations of this pattern, but it was at Palmerston North that I found it with a name. Sports shop proprietor Menzies Hallett told me that this pattern has been tied for a good many years by Mr Leslie Hastings of Palmerston North. It has been on the Taupo scene for many years, especially in the very small sizes when it makes a capital smelt fly. In this case it is loosely referred to as a White Rabbit.

LORD'S KILLER　　　　　　　　　　　　　FRANK LORD
Body: Wool, yellow or red
Tail: Black squirrel
Body feathers: Woodcock plumage, preferably brown rather than buff

Perhaps the best known of all the killer flies, this pattern was the creation of Mr Frank Lord of Rotorua, who tells me that he first made it about 1940. It is a fly-tier's curse, as the soft feathers are not the easiest to tie in nicely, and a good many are used to make a good fly. I have used as many as sixteen to build one to my satisfaction. This, however, is more than compensated by the effective manner in which this pattern takes trout. It works just as effectively on browns as it does on rainbows. One of these flies, well tied and nicely balanced, is a possession to be treasured.

MALLARD AND CLARET　　　　HOOK: 2–8
Tail: Golden pheasant tippets
Body: Claret seal's fur or claret chenille
Rib: Gold oval tinsel
Wing: Bronze mallard
Hackle: Claret

This lure has the same dressing as that used for the smaller wet flies. It has long been recognised as an excellent night fly and is one of the few older patterns that has survived virtually unchanged.

MALLARD LURES　　HOOK: 2–8　　G. SANDERSON
Body: Wool, yellow or red are the favourites although the body colour is nearly always hidden by the side feathers.
Body feathers: The grey breast feathers of a mallard drake
Tail: Black squirrel, or two good grey hackles laid back to back

The mallard lure is a very effective fly on lake-run trout. It is simple to tie and to the shooter there is no shortage of materials. The feathers used are from the breast of a mallard drake. Many prefer the grey hackles in the tail which give the fly a more or less uniformity of colour, but there are those anglers who are emphatic that the fly is better if a tail of squirrel is used. Most prefer black squirrel, while a barred grey squirrel is often used. I must admit that the latter is the dressing I favour.

I have seen it tied with opossum tail, and another variation of the dressing I have come across has the body feathers dyed green, making the fly a very similar pattern to a Hamill's Killer.

The mallard lure was the design of Mr Geoff Sanderson of Turangi, although Mrs Val Galley ties a lure with a cock pheasant tail which she calls a Grey Drake.

MALLARD BLACK (BOSOMWORTH'S)   HOOK: 6–8
E. BOSOMWORTH
Body: Black wool teased out to look a little on the scraggy side and secured with a silver rib
Wing: Several grey mallard feathers laid on top and tied in so that the edges pull nicely down the sides
Tips: Bright orange fibres

This fly is the creation of Eddie Bosomworth, the New Zealand champion flycaster. It is a night fly which fishes well on more moonlit nights: Bosomworth tells me it fishes well at the Rotorua stream mouths when used in conjunction with a floating line.

MALLARD HEN   HOOK: 2–8
Body: Yellow or red
Body feathers: Breast feathers from a mallard hen
Tail: Two nicely marked grizzle hackles laid over the top of two ginger hackles. This gives the tail a mottled colour in keeping with the side feathers.

This is a little-known but very effective lure. It is tied in exactly the same manner as Sanderson's mallard lure, except that the body feathers are those from a mallard hen. This fly has a colouration very close to the natural bully, and is a good fly for either lake or river fishing.

Lures

MALLARD SMELT   HOOK: 6–10
Tail: A narrow strip of mallard drake flank
Body: White floss with silver rib
Hackle: White (tied sparsely)

This pattern is attributed to Mr A. V. (Bruno) Kemball of Hatepe. His shop the "Red Spinner" is well known to Taupo anglers. The Mallard Smelt is an extremely effective fly and is tied with a variation of body colours, green being almost as popular as the white. If white nylon wool is used for dressing the hook, and red or green tying silk used, the colour shows through when the fly is wet; just as the colour of the plankton the smelt feed on shows through the thin walls of their stomachs.

MAORI CHIEF   HOOK: 2–8
Body: Red silk or mohair ribbed with gold
Wing: Bunched fibres from the tail of a cock pheasant
Hackle: Red cock
Tag: The end of a red hen's neck hackle

This is an old Taupo fly that has gone out of fashion. It was one of the transitory patterns that bridged the evolution between the salmon fly and the Taupo fly as we know it today.

MATUKU   HOOK: 2–8
Body: Wool or chenille, colour to liking
Wing: Two soft hen pheasant flank feathers tied in back to back and secured to the body by an oval tinsel ribbing taken through the wings

The original Matuku flies were tied from the feathers of the bittern, "matuku" being the Maori name of this bird. The mottled feathers of the bittern are very soft and work in the current of the stream. Some of the under-rump feathers are a pale cream with a darker coloured stripe down the centre. The bittern has been a protected bird in this country for many years and the importation of bittern skins from other countries is prohibited.

Reluctant to lose these wonderful flies anglers found a substitute in the soft flank feathers of a hen pheasant. Since they were used as a substitute for the matuku any fly tied with them in this manner is now called a Matuku. They are good flies and have stood me in good stead over the years. There was a period for several seasons when

I used little else and I recall one evening with a bag of eleven trout I took on a yellow-bodied Matuku. I would think that the two favoured colours would be yellow and orange although they are tied in many colours. For some reason the Matuku is not used by many anglers these days.

MRS SIMPSON HOOK: 2–8 ANONYMOUS
Tail: Black squirrel tail
Body: Wool (yellow or red)
Side Feathers: The greeny short rump feathers of a cock pheasant

This pattern is the one usually given for Mrs Simpson in most of the catalogues although there is still controversy over its validity. The mystery of the Mrs Simpson goes a long way to illustrating how the origin of many patterns has become confused.

Fred Fletcher tells how the "first" Mrs Simpson was dressed at his lodge at Waitahanui by an Auckland solicitor, Selwyn Clark. Clark used the striped brown feathers from a partridge back to tie his pattern and many Taupo anglers still claim this pattern to be the true Mrs Simpson. This dressing is sold under the name of Kilwell 1.

O. S. Hintz claims that the first Mrs Simpson was the fly known as a Fuzzy Wuzzy and refers to this pattern as such in his book *Trout at Taupo*.

Frank Lord tells me that an angler from Hastings whose name he cannot remember used to breed a strain of mutant pheasants and used the blackish-green feathers to tie the first Mrs Simpson.

I relate elsewhere R. K. Bragg's story of how Miss Mona Carter of Tisdalls tied up another Mrs Simpson from kea feathers.

The Mrs Simpson dressing I have given here is the Kilwell pattern and John Wells Snr of Rotorua told me how his firm came by it. According to Wells a friend of his used to stay at a lodge renowned for its excellent dry fly fishing. The guide often used to go away on his own, returning with a good bag always caught on the "dry". The guest noticed the wet tail of a lure sticking out from under the fold of his cloth cap and when it was hung on a peg he wasted no time in removing the specimen. It had obviously been used very recently and the fly was sent to Wells to be copied. It proved a success and today sells in thousands. Wells called the pattern Mrs Simpson.

All these little anecdotes just go to show how time has spun some good stories concerning the beginnings of lure and fly origins.

MRS SIMPSON (KEA)   HOOK: 4–8   MONA CARTER

In 1939 a fisherman brought a kea skin into Tisdalls' Christchurch branch and asked for some flies to be made from it. One of Tisdalls' tiers, a Miss Mona Carter, made up a lure of the feathers and called it Mrs Simpson. This pattern is still sold in some South Island shops under this name, although I have more often come across it known as a Kea fly. It is tied in the normal killer fashion with a black squirrel tail, although a red feather from under the bird's wing is used as a tail overlay.

NAILER   HOOK: 2–6   R. NAYLOR
Wing: Turkey
Body: Chenille in four segments of alternate black and yellow
Tag: Silver
Tail: Tippets
Hackle: Black cock
Cheeks: The lesser coverts of a hen pheasant wing

I believe that this fly should really be called the Naylor after its inventor Mr R. Naylor, who was an angler on the Taupo scene for many years. After he had tied the original it was lost in the jaw of a trout which was caught several days later by another angler. The fly was sent to Kelly's in Rotorua and appears in one of their old pattern sheets. This fly is not to be found in the shops today, but I include its dressing because of its historical significance.

OPOSSUM LURE   HOOK: 2–8
Body: Yellow chenille
Wing: A strip of yellow opossum belly with fur attached
Whisks: Red (dyed)

This is a pattern that is not often come across, but it has its adherents nevertheless. It is tied from the belly of an opossum skin and a strip of skin with fur attached is tied in exactly the same way on a rabbit fly.

I believe this fly is popular on Lake Tarawera, especially at the outlet. I have an angling friend for whom I have tied quite a lot of these flies for his annual pilgrimage to the "outlet". He favours the fly in the very small sizes and claims they are extremely effective.

ORANGE WITCH   HOOK: 4–8   P. LAING
Tail: Black Squirrel
Body: Orange chenille
Side feather: Barred flanks from chukor

This fly is effective in the early part of the season but for some reason it loses its appeal after Christmas. Early morning, evening and night fly. One angler at Ellesmere in 1966 took forty-nine fish in eight trips. The angler fished two flies, one always a Witch. He used about twenty other patterns for the other lure, alternating at the tail and the dropper. The Witch accounted for forty-eight of the trout taken. The fly is unlikely to become common as the feathers are difficult to obtain, the chukor living high among the mountains. It is also effective on landlocked salmon and rainbows.

ORBIT (*GREEN, RED AND YELLOW*)   HOOK: 2–8
                                                       W. BEAUMONT-ORR
GREEN ORBIT:
Body: Green wool, fur or chenille
Ribbing: Gold
Wing and Hackles: Grizzle hackle dyed green

This fly was the design of the late Wilfred Beaumont-Orr, a fly tier and tackle retailer who operated in Taupo before the Second World War. The name of the fly is a play on the surname of the originator.

The Green Orbit is a good fly, especially at night, but in the smaller sizes it will often kill well during daylight hours. In the summer you will often find fish with a fair amount of green weed in their stomachs and some anglers claim that this is why the trout prefer the Orbit. I have yet to be fully convinced as I have yet to see a piece of weed swimming upstream against the current, but there can be no denying it is a good fly. The dyeing of the grizzle feathers often covers a wide range of tints from deep emerald green to a lime-hued colour, but whatever the shade of green they are still an Orbit.

Not so well known as the Green Orbit but equally as effective are the Red Orbit and the Yellow. They are tied with grizzle feathers dyed to the correct colour, the body material being the same colour as the feather.

The Yellow Orbit is an excellent trolling fly and the red is favoured by some anglers as a night fly. I have noticed some Orange Orbits in one or two tackle shops but I think this is a later development. No doubt colour changes could be made until every shade of the rainbow was employed.

PARSON'S GLORY   HOOK: 2–10   PHIL PARSONS
Body: Yellow chenille or wool
Wing: Honey grizzle neck hackles
Hackle: Honey grizzle neck hackles
Whisks: Red or orange fibres

This fly was the brainchild of Mr Phil Parsons, who farmed near Te Awamutu. He was one of the old Taupo brigade and I think that as long as trout swim in New Zealand his memory will be perpetuated by this fly. It is the golden fly, both in colour and quality, and there can be no doubt that it is the most favoured of all lures for daylight fishing. I think a lot of its success depends on the well-marked honey grizzle feathers used for its wing. Next time you hook a fingerling trout take a good look at his sides before you tenderly release him and you will see the parr blotches along his side, just like a well-marked honey grizzle feather.

You will come across a few variations in the Parson's Glory. Some prefer a very pale buff-coloured feather while others like a gingery hackle. Some prefer a rough wool body and others a slim one. Whatever the individual's preference the basic ingredients remain the same. Plate 1 shows two Parson's Glorys. The first was tied by Mr O. S. Hintz and is a replica of the first style of fly tied by Parsons himself. This fly is still under the influence of the salmon fly, hence the gold tag, mohair body and sweeping crown of golden pheasant topping. And in those days no-one would think of tying a fly without using jungle cock.

The second is the style favoured by most anglers today. It has a heavier body and is fairly solid, deadliest when tied on smaller sizes, even as small as No. 10.

POTT'S PET HOOK: 2–6
Body: Yellow wool with an orange tag
Wing: Bronze peacock herl
Side cheeks: Lesser coverts from a hen pheasant wing
Ribbing: Gold tinsel

Gwynne Potts was the Taupo district ranger for many years and was as well known as an angler as a game law enforcer. The fly has passed from the scene today, but had its adherents thirty or more years ago.

RABBIT FLY
Body: Wool or chenille, colour to suit
Wing: A strip of rabbit pelt with the ends nicely tapered
Ribbing: Oval tinsel
Tag: A few whisks of dyed cock hackle, red or yellow
Hackle: To suit, but usually tied to match the body colour. For yellow and orange-bodied flies a pale hackle is used, whereas for night patterns a black or claret hackle looks well

Here perhaps is the best fly of its type in this country. There are possibly more claimants to the invention of the Rabbit Fly than any other pattern, but the oldest supported claim I know of is that of Alan Duncum of Napier. He tells of the time in 1932 when he was fishing down the Waikato — about where Reid's Farm camping reserve is now. During a shower he sheltered under a bush with a Maori angler who had in his tobacco tin a large fly made with a dark hair wing and a red body. The Maori claimed it was a great night fly and Duncum later anxious to try it — snipped some black rabbit fur and pelt from his wife's new slippers. It was tied as a night fly and met with great success. Flies tied from grey rabbit skins were tried with the same result. and today they are sold in their thousands. I myself consider the Rabbit Fly to be the best lure of its type when fishing for lake-run trout. The soft fur works and ripples with every nuance of current and the skin soon softens in the water.

There are several variations of the Rabbit Fly, but they are all based on using a strip of rabbit skin. The fly can be tied on as small as size 8 or even 10, and in this form of tie it makes a very good fly for smelting. Tied heavy the fly can be used as an imitation bully and to help enhance this appearance two cheeks of hen pheasant feathers can be tied in alongside the body. I can vouch for this method of tying and have taken many fish on it over the years.

Some anglers prefer the black rabbit for night and evening fishing but as anyone who has tied these flies will tell you, the rabbit fur is only black on the tips. The underfur is a pale blue or even almost white at times, so to make a really black "Rabbit" fly other furs are sometimes used. If you have any friends who make their living by trapping opossums ask them if they ever take any black cats. The feral cat is often taken by opossum trappers, which is a good thing, as these predators take a large toll of game and wildlife. The skin of a black cat with its thick pelage of winter fur makes excellent flies, but remember that it is illegal to trade in them. Promise your trapper friend a nice trout in exchange for a cat skin.

With a rabbit skin several parts of the pelt will give a different colour. The fur varies from a black flecked with brown to a pale grey or even pure white if the skin has a good belly. For the body wool, chenille or seal's fur can be used. It makes little difference which is used, so long as the angler is happy with it. I myself prefer dyed seal's fur as it glistens so well in the sunlight. One often thinks that it could sometimes be small considerations such as these which induce a sulky trout to strike.

RED SETTER: HOOK: 2–8 G. SANDERSON
Body: Orange chenille or wool
Tail: Bunched brown or ginger squirrel tail
Hackle: Usually tied with two large ginger hackles, one at the head, the other tied in halfway along the body. In the smallest sizes one hackle can be used while on the extra large hooks three or even four are sometimes tied in.

This fly is one of the best there is for taking lake-run trout. It is tied in the same manner as a fuzzy wuzzy and is the creation of Mr Geoff Sanderson of Turangi. The fly often fishes well after dark.

RED SHADOW   HOOK: 2–8   R. K. BRAGG
Body: White chenille, with silver ribbing
Wing: Two dyed red hackles laid over black hackles
Hackle: Black

Here is a Canterbury pattern that enjoys a great deal of popularity in Rotorua. It is a night fly at its best and while I have never used it, I have met some anglers who are prepared to swear by it.

RED TERROR
Body: Red
Wing and Hackle: Red (dyed)
Rib: Silver
Overlay: Green Peacock
  Jungle Cock

This pattern is regarded as a night lure and is really a handsome variation of the Cardinal. It is a Canterbury lure.

ROYAL TAN   HOOK: 2–8   R. K. BRAGG
Whisks: Red
Body: Yellow chenille
Wing: Grizzle hackles dyed deep golden yellow
Hackle: Grizzle hackles dyed deep golden yellow

This pattern is a variation of the Parson's Glory, although it should really be classed as a version of the Yellow Orbit.

When W. Beaumont-Orr designed his Orbits the yellow never reached the popularity of its green brother, so it is understandable how Bragg came to evolve his dressing.

The Royal Tan sold quite well on the Rotorua scene, as Bragg used to dress the flies for one of that town's retailers.

SALMON FLIES

Apart from the traditional salmon flies that have now gone out of use anglers in the South Island have found that the Quinnat salmon (*Onchorhynchus tschawytcha*) will take a fly more readily

Lures

than was once thought. Large variations of the more popular patterns are used, some of the favourites being Parson's Glory, Taupo Tiger, Hart Creek, Hope's Dark, etc. I am told that the larger, darker patterns are preferred in the glacial-fed rivers with their milky waters, but in rivers such as the Ashburton where cleaner waters are to be found, the lighter-coloured dressings on smaller hooks prove quite successful.

SCOTCH POACHER: HOOK: 2–8 J. KIRKPATRICK
Body: Orange chenille with gold ribbing
Tail: Black squirrel
Wing: Blue pukeko tied Craig style
Hackle: Orange

Jock Kirkpatrick of Rotorua designed this lure. Bill Hamill tells me that he always calls Kirkpatrick "an old Scotch poacher" by way of a joke. When the fly became a commercial proposition the name was a foregone conclusion. This pattern has taken some parts of the country by storm and is an excellent night lure. It was this dressing that Tom Wall of Waitahanui used one March night in 1968, when he landed a beautiful hen brown trout of $19\frac{1}{2}$ pounds.

SILVER DOCTOR HOOK: 2–8
Body: Flat silver tinsel ribbed with silver thread
Wing: Grey mallard flank
Hackle: Pale blue
Tail: Tippets

This fly is a relic from the days of the salmon fly. It is still used to good effect in many parts of the country and is to be considered as a good early-season fly. There can be little doubt that it is taken by trout as some small form of fry. The pattern used today is a simplification of the more colourful original. The salmon fly dressed in full regalia uses a wing of strips of goose dyed red, yellow and green then overlaid with grey mallard flank. All the fancy petticoats have been dropped and our modern version has a wing of grey mallard only. I suspect that it is none the worse for it.

SILVER SMELT   HOOK: 4–8
Body: Silver tinsel
Wing: Nylon hair, white on green dyed
Eye: White with black centre

This pattern has been made very popular by the Rotorua firm of W. Hamill. It is a very close imitation of a smelt and is greatly enhanced by the eye.

SNAIL FLY   HOOK: 8–10   F. LORD
Body: Black
Wing: Pukeko
Topping: A good curl of green peacock sword herl

Created by Mr Frank Lord of Rotorua this fly is intended to copy more or less the shape of a freshwater snail. It is fished slowly on a floating line and is very effective, according to its designer. As any angler who has fished a lake where freshwater snails abound will know, these molluscs can form an important part of the trout's diet. There are two types of water snails, operculate, which extract oxygen from the water and pulmonate, which have to come to the surface occasionally to fill their single lung. It is probably one of these latter species that Lord's fly imitates so successfully. The idea is an ingenious one, but Frank Lord has long enjoyed a reputation as an ingenious angler.

SPA SPECIAL   HOOK: 2–8
Body: Yellow mohair ribbed with silver
Side feather: Grey partridge tied in each side
Tail: A bunch of fibres from a grey turkey feather

The Spa Special is a stablemate of the Leslie's Lure. It was designed by Mr Leslie Newdick who was once host of the Spa Hotel in Taupo. The hotel has riparian rights over some of the Waikato River which flows close by and the Spa Special will kill just as well there today as it did over thirty years ago, although the river no longer holds the same head of fish. Fluctuating levels caused by hydro-electric development have greatly ruined this river as a fishery. I have not seen a Spa Special in a tackle shop for years, but I know personally what a great lure it can be.

Lures

SPLIT PARTRIDGE   HOOK: 2–8
Body: Chenille or wool, with oval tinsel rib
Wing: Split partridge tail
Hackle: Brown cock
Tag: Dyed fibres from cock hackle

Here is a good fly that is unfortunately on the way out. This is not because it is losing its popularity, but because the supply of good partridge tails becomes less certain with each passing season. Those that are obtainable cost a small fortune. Be this as it may the partridge is a great fly. Barney Northcroft of Waitahanui, widely known for his ability with the fly rod, claims that for rip fishing in the lake there is no better fly. I don't know who invented this pattern but the late Fred Fletcher told of Wilfred Harbutt of Cambridge who nearly forty years ago used to send to Hardy's of Alnwick to have his split partridges tied. The tail feather of a partridge is split down the centre and the two matching sides cut from out of the feather. The fibres are still attached to the spines and these are held to the body with the ribbing being taken through the feather and binding the spine to the fly.

SQUIRREL

I have come across this name several times but the pattern is nothing less than a hairy dog, though to be fair it must be admitted that a true hairy dog should be tied from dog hair. However, it has long been customary to tie a Hairy Dog with squirrel tail so I think that it has prior claim to the name.

SQUIRREL NUTKIN   HOOK: 2–8   R. K. BRAGG
Tail: Brown hackle points
Body: Flat gold tinsel
Wing: Brown squirrel
Hackle: Brown

This pattern is Bragg's variation of a Demon Squirrel. This style of fly is highly regarded the world over where large trout and fast waters are to be found.

STRING FLY   HOOK: 8–10
Tail: Piece of white string or jute from a sugar bag
Body: White wool with silver ribbing

    This pattern is so simple many anglers would consider it to be an insult to a trout's intelligence. Be that as it may, the string fly is extremely effective when trout are smelting. Mr Tom Hope, a Taupo angler of repute, is well known as an exponent of the pattern and has taken countless trout on it over the years.

    Taxi Kapua, Borough Councillor and Maori elder, tells me that the pattern is especially effective where the hot Waipahihi stream flows into Lake Taupo. The smelt sometimes swim into the hot water and are cooked, turning white. Kapua claims that a white string fly drifted along the edge of the current is deadly when a school of trout are in the bay.

SWAGGER   HOOK: 2–8   D. HOPE
Tail: Barred Rock
Body: White with flat embossed silver tinsel
Hackle: Barred Rock
Wing: Black orpington
Cheeks: Paradise duck on either side

    This pattern is a variation of the Hope's Dark with the addition of the paradise duck cheeks. Another successful Canterbury fly.

SWEEP   HOOK: 2–8   R. K. BRAGG
Body: Black chenille ribbed with gold oval tinsel
Wings: Black orpington with side feathers of white hen dyed Kingfisher blue
Hackle: Black

    A Canterbury lure, first designed in 1949, the creation of Mr R. K. Bragg of Christchurch.

TAIHAPE TICKLER: HOOK: 2–8   F. LORD
Body: Claret chenille
Wing: Blue pukeko feathers
Hackle: Claret cock

Rotorua's Frank Lord was responsible for the Tickler and the story of its origin is typical of how many flies came to be and how they came to be named. Lord, who ran a sports shop for many years, decided he would make up a special night fly. Knowing that the Craig's Night-time and the Mallard and Claret were two good night flies he combined the body and hackle of the Mallard and Claret with a pukeko wing such as that used in a Craig's. He set off to the mouth of the Awahou one night and in short order caught his limit of fish. As he was pulling out, Chris Christophers, who was hatchery manager of Ngongataha, arrived. He gave the fly to Christophers to use and while they were talking another angler who had been fishing close by came and joined them. It was Bert Jensen who came from Taihape and he wanted to know what fly Lord had used to catch all his fish. Shown the fly, he commented, "By crikey, that's a real Taihape Tickler", and that is how it came to get its name.

TAIL-LIGHT   HOOK: 2–8
Body: Black chenille
Hackle: Two large black hackles, one tied into the body, the other at the head
Tail: A large tag of bright red wool

This fly was designed to deal with fish that are taking short. This often happens at night and especially so with the brown trout that come into the river-mouths in the summer nights. Their soft slow take often makes it difficult to get a hook into their jaw. This abbreviated version of the Fuzzy Wuzzy helps to overcome this tendency.

TAMATI   HOOK: 2–8
Body: Three segments of red, black and yellow chenille
Wing: Split grouse or partridge
Hackle: Red
Whisks: Yellow

Tamati was an old Maori who lived at Waipahihi, Taupo. The bay now known as Two Mile Bay was once called Tamati's Bay. There he kept a boat for hire, with himself as boatman. It is said that when devising this fly he used the ragwort moth for inspiration, and the body of his fly was made up in four segments of black and yellow, each one having a red hackle wound in between. A tag of silver was used, a relic from salmon fly dressings, with a tail of golden pheasant topping. The wing was turkey and jungle cock cheeks finished the fly. It hardly looks like a ragwort moth, especially as it was usually tied on a No. 2 or 1/0 hook, but it did catch trout. That was the original dressing and it disappeared from the scene about twenty years ago. The fly sold under the name today bears little resemblance to Tamati's creation, but those oldtimers who personally knew the old Maori are pleased that at least his name is perpetuated; he was a great old fisherman.

TAUPO TIGER (OR *TIGER ROSS*)   HOOK: 2–8   J. ROSS
Body: Yellow with silver ribbing
Wing: Badger hackles, with a good black centre
Hackle: Badger
Whisks: Red
Head: Red

This fly which would run a very close second to the Parson's Glory in popularity, was the design of James Ross, who ran a tobacco and tackle business in Napier. He invented the Tiger about 1930, and being in the business he was determined to keep the retail rights of the fly to himself. He could not patent the dressing as it was readily available to anyone, but he was able to obtain a registered trade name. This did not worry the opposition in the least, as they just gave the fly another name — the Taupo Tiger — and they were quite within their legal rights. It is only correct though to give credit where it is due and Ross's fly has been a consistent fish taker for forty years. It is my experience that the fly is used more by trollers and harlers than by stream fishermen. Tied on a very small hook it is an excellent fly to use when the trout are smelting.

Lures

TONGARIRO QUEEN HOOK: 2–6
Body: Four segments of chenille in alternate red and yellow. Ginger hackles tied in between each segment
Tag: Silver
Tail: Golden pheasant topping
Wing: Turkey

This is another fly that has disappeared with the passage of time.

TUBE FLIES

The Tube Fly style of lure is being used by some anglers in New Zealand, but they have not yet become popular. I think they are worthy of inclusion here because they might become fashionable in time.

The principle is extremely simple and consists merely of a small plastic or light metal tube dressed with fur, hair or feather. They are becoming very popular in Britain, where they are used for salmon and sea trout. The tube is slid up the cast and a small treble hook attached. The lure then sits back on the hook. I have dressed some of these flies and seen many illustrations of those used overseas. I have been greatly struck by their similarity to some of our Taupo lures. Geoff Sanderson's Dappled Dog is very close to some of these patterns. No doubt there will be many home fly tiers who will want to try these patterns. They cannot be used in waters where multiple hooks are illegal.

TURKEY (YELLOW AND RED) HOOK: 2–6
Body: Thick wool or mohair, usually yellow or red
Wing: Brown turkey, tied long and swept back
Tail: A bunch of brown turkey, the tail ending under the long wing tip
Hackle: Long soft red cock

Once upon a time no respectable Taupo angler would be without his Turkeys, be they reds or yellows. These large flies were one of the most popular styles for many years and their reputation was justly deserved. Somewhere along the way they fell out of favour, relics of the transitory stage of fly development after the salmon fly had passed on. The old ties were large and had a rough look. This appearance was a carefully cultivated one, and to tie a bunch of consistently rough-looking flies takes more skill than is generally credited. Thick-tufted bodies of wool or mohair were normally used.

A later development of the Turkey was the split tie and in most cases the feather used was split grouse tail, but this mode of tying has also nearly disappeared. Both styles of tying are shown in Plate 1.

WAIHORA   HOOK: 2–6   T. RICKIT
Body: Black wool or chenille
Wing: Turkey
Hackle: Black
Whisks: Red

This fly was the design of Tom Rickit of Taupo, who many years ago served as a guide to Zane Grey on some of his fishing trips to New Zealand. It is a night fly and while not much in evidence today still has its adherents. Plate 2.

WARDEN'S WORRY   HOOK: 2–8   KILWELL
Body: Wool, yellow or red with silver tinsel rib
Wing: The long rusty rump feathers of a cock pheasant topped with green peacock sword
Tail: Brown squirrel

A Rotorua fly that has on occasions lived up to its title. It is my experience that in the Taupo area at least it is rather more favoured as a trolling fly.

WILLIS SMELT   HOOK: 4–8
Body: Flat silver tinsel with oval rib
Wing: A pair of small white satins from the underside of a wild duck's wing
Eye: Yellow eyes on black head

This simple pattern is used by W. Willis of Te Kuiti. I have one small criticism to make of this particular fly — it is a little on the stiff side. However, its creator points out that it has the distinct advantage of never wrapping around the hook as do some flies tied with softer feathers.

Lures

WOOLLY WORM: HOOK: 2–8
Body: Chenille, colour to suit. Favoured shades orange and green
Hackle: Usually grizzle, tied palmerwise
Tail: Usually just the tip of a hackle feather

This is a style of fly that is generally tied on a large hook and fished as a lure in the northern lakes area. That it resembles a worm is rather questionable, but there can be no doubt about its effectiveness.

WOOSTER'S SILVERY HOOK: 2–8 W. WOOSTER
Body: White
Wing: Ginger with grey mallard overlay
Hackle: Ginger

I have dressed this pattern (Plate 2) in the modern slim manner rather than the heavy bulky type of tie common to the South Island lure. The lighter style of dressing is more effective, especially when casting to trout that are feeding on smelt or whitebait.

WOOSTER'S SILVERY RED HOOK: 2–8
Body: Red
Wing: Ginger with grey mallard overlay
Hackle: Ginger

YELLOW TERROR HOOK: 2–8 R. K. BRAGG
Butt: A turn of fluorescent red chenille
Body: Silver tinsel with a yellow hackle wound palmerwise along the body
Wing: Yellow (dyed) cock hackle ribbed with silver
Hackle: Yellow

A bright Canterbury lure and considered by some to be a good pattern for coloured water.

PLATE 1

Taupo and Rotorua lures

1. Turkey and Red (old tie). **2.** Tamati (old tie). **3.** Potts Pet (obsolete).

4. Turkey and Red (modern). **5.** Tamati (modern). **6.** Mallard and Claret (old tie).

7. Ewe Wasp. **8.** Waihora. **9.** Mallard and Claret (modern). **10.** Golden Demon.

11. Matuku, Yellow. **12.** Spa Special. **13.** Leslies Lure.

14. Parson's Glory (original tie). **15.** Parson's Glory (modern).

16. Taupo Tiger or Tiger Ross. **17.** Red Split Partridge. **18.** Yellow Dorothy.

19. Yellow Hawk. **20.** Red Hairy Dog. **21.** Green Orbit. **22.** Red Ferris.

23. Ginger Mick. **24.** Jack's Sprat. **25.** Bishop's Blessing. **26.** Red Setter.

27. Furry Butcher. **28.** Keeler. **29.** Warden's Worry. **30.** Green Woolly Worm.

31. Mrs Simpson. **32.** Lord's Killer. **33.** Hamill's Killer. **34.** Kilwell No. 1.

35. Kilwell No. 2. **36.** Brown Killer. **37.** Mallard (squirrel tail).

38. Mallard (grey tail).

PLATE 2

Night lures, Canterbury lures, smelt flies, fur flies and specials

Some night lures

1. Fuzzy Wuzzy.   **2.** Black Phantom.   **3.** Guardsman.   **4.** Taihape Tickler.
5. Craigs Night time.   **6.** Scotch Poacher.   **7.** Snail Fly.   **8.** Black Mallard.

Some Canterbury lures

9. Hope's Silvery White.   **10.** Hope's Silvery Red.   **11.** Christie.   **12.** Red Terror.
13. Devil Dodger.   **14.** Yellow Bully.   **15.** Mrs Simpson Kea.   **16.** Hope's Dark.
17. Sweep.   **18.** Yellow Terror.   **19.** Hart Creek.   **20.** Red Shadow.
21. Red Barred Rock.   **22.** Orange Witch.   **23.** Badger.   **24.** Wooster's Silvery.
25. Brunton Red.

Some Smelt Flies

26. Blue Mallard.   **27.** Mallard & White.   **28.** Silver Hawk and Rabbit.
29. Grey Ghost.   **30.** Blondie.   **31.** Hamill's Smelt.   **32.** Ginger Smelt.
33. Gold Bucktail.   **34.** Mylar Bodied Bucktail.   **35.** Willis Smelt.

Some Fur Flies

36. Yellow Rabbit.   **37.** Black Bugs Bunny.   **38.** Black Rabbit.

Some Specials

39. Jock Miller.   **40.** Hilda.

PLATE 3

Wet Flies and Nymphs

Captain Hamilton's five
1. Red Hackle. 2. Black Hackle. 3. Hare's Ear. 4. Hare's Ear Spider. 5. Black Spider.

Some favourite wet flies and other patterns
6. Red Tipped Governor. 7. Peveril o'the Peak. 8. Coachman. 9. Jessie 1. 10 Jessie 2
11. Heckham Peckam. 12. Bradshaw's Fancy. 13. Hardy's Favourite.
14. Hofland's Fancy. 15. White Moth. 16. Stonefly (mallard).
17. Stonefly (pheasant). 18. Claret March Brown. 19. Red Spinner.
20. Purple Grouse. 21. Orange Woodcock. 22. Invicta. 23. Thompson's Moth.
24. Temuka. 25. Red Paradise. 26. Green Beetle. 27. Brown Beetle.
28. Dickinson's Beetle. 29. Black Beetle. 30. Love's Lure. 31. Black Spinner.
32. Green Caterpillar. 33. Golden Shrimp. 34. Brown Dragon Nymph.
35. Bragg's Dragon Nymph.

Nymphs
36. Red Nymph. 37. Olive Nymph. 38. Coachman Nymph.
39. Red Tipped Governor Nymph. 40. Hare & Copper. 41. Morris's Hare & Copper.
42. Black. 43. Brown. 44. Grey. 45. Pheasant Tail. 46. October Brown.
47. Opossum Tail. 48. Horn Caddis Nymph. 49. Stone Caddis. 50. Ginger Quill.
51. Black Gnat. 52. Laing's Quill. 53. Laing's Furry. 54. Late Spring Olive.
55. Skue's Blue Dun. 56. Early Spring Olive. 57. Mayfly. 58. Green & Red.
59. Furry Black. 60. Peacock & Copper. 61. Peacook & Purple.
62. Peacock & Green. 63. Peacock & Black. 64. March Brown.
65. March Brown Midget. 66. Perla Nymph. 67. Green Stonefly. 68. Blue Ritz.
69. Orange Nymph. 70. Bragg's Horn Caddis. 71. Pye's Sedge Nymph.

PLATE 4

Dry Flies

Some old favourites and many new patterns

1. Peveril o'the Peak. 2. Coachman. 3. Red Tipped Governor. 4. Hunt's Favourite.
5. March Brown. 6. Blue Dun. 7. Dad's Favourite. 8. Hare's Ear.
9. Hardy's Favourite. 10. Molefly. 11. West Coast Beetle. 12. Coch-y-Bondhu.
13. Bragg's Blue Bottle. 14. Dean's Black Gnat. 15. Relish. 16. Love's Lure.
17. Green Beetle (Morris's). 18. Brown Beetle (Morris's). 19. Hutton's Beetle.
20. Black Palmer (Morris's). 21. Turkey Sedge. 22. Speckled Sedge. 23. Invicta
24. Red Palmer. 25. Studholme's Greenwell. 26. Bi-visible. 27. Pheasant Tail.
28. Murray's Favourite. 29. Kakahi Queen. 30. Twilight Beauty.
31. Greenwell (dark). 32. Greenwell (light). 33. Brer Rabbit. 34. Bragg's Blue Dun.
35. Twilight Beauty (Canterbury). 36. Bragg's Early Olive Dun.
37. Black winged Dun (Mottram). 38. Red Quill Hackle. 39. Black Spinner.
40. Wickham's Fancy. 41. Summer Dun (Morris's). 42. Red Spinner.
43. Dark Red Quill (spent). 44. Welham's Red Spinner. 45. Laing's Twilight.
46. Damsel Fly (red). 47. Lace Moth (Willis's) 48. Blue Spinner (spent).
49. Mottram's Mayfly (spinner). 50. Parachute Spinner (dark spinner).
51. Parachute Spinner (Coachman).

3
WET AND DRY FLIES

The history of wet and dry flies in New Zealand has moved in a more orthodox manner than the lures. The vast majority of the former are imported from the United Kingdom and with the exception of those patterns peculiar to this country, they are nearly all the standard patterns that are to be found in the United Kingdom. For that reason I have included in this section a good number of dressings that are not well known but because of their divergence from the commercial group of patterns, deserve recognition. Many of these flies fill gaps in the commercial range. There are some New Zealand anglers who have developed their fly fishing to a very exacting art and I hope that some of the following patterns will help to prove this point.

Of historical interest is the inclusion of the wet patterns of Captain G. D. Hamilton and the dries of Dr J. C. Mottram.

Hamilton, who had a large home on the banks of the Manawatu river near Dannevirke, seems to have been the pioneer of trout acclimatisation in the North Island. In the early 1870s he had brown trout ova from the South Island transported more than fifty miles by packhorse to where he had built a private hatchery on the Mangatoro Stream, a tributary of the Manawatu. Within three years he was catching trout and the five Tweedside flies he used are described under "Captain Hamilton's Flies".

Hamilton wrote of New Zealand angling in his book *Trout Fishing and Sport in Maoriland*, published by the Government Printing Office, Wellington, in 1904. The captain was a practical Scot and I don't doubt a book of this nature would have filled him with horror.

He wrote, among other things that . . . "the multiplication of the varieties of flies used is one of the ways of making a complicated business of what is really a simple matter".

He also raises a point many of us would do well to ponder on. "It often happens that where a great variety of flies and minnows is used a change in the fly or minnow fished with gets the credit of obtaining better sport when the credit should be given to the altered humour of the fish — to their coming on to feed." Wise words indeed and just as applicable today as they were a century ago.

Hamilton was a wet fly fisherman and dismissed dry fly fishing:

"Whatever its merits under exceptional conditions, it has the disadvantage that in ordinary circumstances the fly spends most of its time in the air instead of on the water. To those who care to familiarise themselves with this mode of fishing I would recommend among many others a newly published book *Dry Fly Fishing* by F. M. Halford where this subject occupies as many pages as are in the whole of this book (Hamilton's). I must not, however, be understood to endorse the great number of flies mentioned."

The good captain, then, would have had little in common with Dr J. C. Mottram who was probably the first dry fly angler on the New Zealand scene. It appears he fished in the Canterbury area within a decade of trout having been established there, probably in the 1880s.

G B. Hobbs in *Fisherman's Country* published by Geoffrey Bles of London in 1955, gives as an appendix Mottram's dressings of New Zealand mayflies outlined in the latter's book *Fly-fishing, Some New Arts and Mysteries*, published in 1915.

I have included some of Mottram's dressings but they cannot be taken as popular patterns. Indeed, Mrs Alice Harmer, a professional fly-tier, employed by Tisdalls of Christchurch, says that she has been asked to dress Mottram's flies on no more than several occasions, and in each case without a repeat order. Mrs Harmer, who trained in England, is held by many South Island anglers to be one of the finest fly-tiers in the country.

Dry fly fishing is being developed to a very high art in some parts of the country, especially so in the lovely province of Southland. The latitude allows a long gloaming in the summer evenings and the area is well blessed with members of the Ephemeridae. I have fished in Southland on several occasions but always late in the season, and the weather was against the conditions required for a good hatch. Some of the southern rivers, more particularly the Mataura, are developing a reputation that is attracting dry fly anglers from all over the world. For many years these fine and gentle waters have been ignored by the publicity given to the North Island lakes district where, incidentally, excellent small fly fishing is again overshadowed by the popularity of lure fishing for the large lake-grown rainbows.

It is to be hoped that in this section the reader will find some patterns that will help him in outwitting the wily trout of his own favourite stream or lake.

ALDER   WET AND DRY   HOOK: 8–14
Wing: Brown speckled hen's wing quill, tied penthouse
Body: Bronze peacock herl
Hackle: Black

The artificial Alder copies an English insect of the Neutropera order. The member of the Neuroptera family with which all New Zealand anglers are familiar has as its larva that wellknown insect the creeper, often called the toe-biter or dobson fly. The adult form, commonly known as the lacewing, bears little resemblance to the English variety, so the fly pattern given here is not a fair representation of its New Zealand counterpart. But the English pattern will kill New Zealand trout quite readily, and in some districts is a much-favoured pattern. Since it is tied with penthouse wings and is usually most effective at dusk it is probably taken for a sedge. The New Zealand alder (*Archichauliodes diversus*) more closely resembles an elongated sedge shape, ($1\frac{3}{4}$ in. long) the English species being a much dumpier insect.

I have come across no New Zealand artificial fly tied to copy the indigenous alder, although one of the stonefly patterns given elsewhere bears a strong superficial resemblance to it.

ALEXANDRA   WET   HOOK: 8–14
Wing: Green peacock herl
Body: Flat silver tinsel
Tail: Red ibis or dyed feather strip
Hackle: Black

A good all-round fly of English origin, first used about 1860 and named after Queen Alexandra. While this pattern was intended primarily as a brown and sea trout pattern it is effective on rainbows. It can also be tied on a larger hook as a salmon fly and was often used in the Taupo area in the early days dressed on large No. 2 and 4 hooks. This fly is sometimes called the Alexander, and while small variations in the pattern occur from time to time the above is the correct and proper dressing.

ANT FLIES

In New Zealand we have about twenty species of ants, all of which at some stage of their cycles produce winged specimens. This enables them to spread and proliferate. After mating the males die, the females shedding their wings to start a new colony. The worker ants, which are sexless, do not have wings.

Most New Zealand anglers will agree that ants do not constitute a very important item on the trout's menu. However, those that inadvertently end up in the water are not ignored, as I have found the odd one in autopsies. In Australia ants are a common insect and are often found on the water. The Australians have therefore developed several fly patterns based on the flying ants. The bodies are built up of floss or some similar material and comprise two sections, the thorax and abdomen, with a couple of turns of hackle wound between. I have seen some specimens that were lacquered to give a shiny appearance, and I know one angler (an expatriate Australian) who has used them with some success in New Zealand.

BADGER PALMER DRY HOOK: 8–14
Tail: Tips of badger hackle
Body: Black tying thread
Hackle: Badger hackle of a creamy colour
Rib: Silver wire

J. Morris describes this pattern as being ideal, along with the other palmer flies, to use on the dropper with a nymph used on the point.

BAY DUN (DARK) DRY HOOK: 10–16
Whisks: Furnace
Body: Strands of cock pheasant tail secured with fine copper rib
Hackle: Dark furnace

BAY DUN (LIGHT) DRY HOOK: 10–16
Whisks: Ginger
Body: Pheasant tail secured with fine copper ribbing
Hackle: Ginger

Both the above dressings were named thus by the late J. Morris. They are really variations of the pheasant tail. Morris was a Bay of Plenty angler, hence the "Bay" prefix to the Duns. This slight case of parochialism can be easily excused. To many "Bay" anglers Morris was the *doyen* of the gentle art.

Wet and Dry Flies

BEETLE SERIES
BROWN BEETLE   DRY   HOOK: 10–14
Body: Brown wool
Wing cases: Cock pheasant tail fibres
Hackle: Brown cock (short tail, optional)
   A Canterbury pattern.

GREEN BEETLE   WET AND DRY   HOOK: 10–14
Body: Fawn wool
Wing cases: Green floss silk
Hackle: Bright ginger cock hackle for dry, hen for wet
   or
Body: Rabbit fur dubbing   HOOK: 10–14
Wing cases: Green herl from peacock sword feather
Hackle: Bright ginger cock hackle for dry, hen for wet

BROWN BEETLE   WET AND DRY   HOOK: 10–14
Body: Fawn wool
Wing cases: Brown floss silk
Hackle: Natural red cock for dry, hen for wet
   An alternative pattern is:
Body: Rabbit fur dubbing spun on to the tying thread
Wing cases: A strip from the secondary quill feathers of a paradise duck
Hackle: Natural red cock for dry, hen for wet

The brown quill feather for the wing cases can also be found in the wings of some species of domestic fowl. For those with a shotgun a paradise duck presents no problem in the shooting season.

BEETLE FLY (DICKINSON'S — DEER HAIR)   WET AND DRY
HOOK: 12–14

R. Dickinson in his book *Rising Fish* (Whitcombe & Tombs) gives us the following pattern which I have tied and used with success. A small bunch of deer hair is taken and laid along a hook shank with the butts level with the eye. It is tied in about $\frac{1}{8}$ in. back from the eye and whipped and glued into the bend. The butts are then bent out at right angles to the shank and the tail of hair pulled over and tied in at the head. The hair is trimmed off level and the head finished. The butts are then trimmed up to represent legs. Tied like this the underview of the fly looks somewhat rough, but the fish take it well. To hide the whipped shank the hook can be dubbed with rabbit fur or velvet chenille. This gives a more finished-looking article. Its creator suggests painting its back with bright green nail polish and goes on to say that the fly should not be oiled, as it will float best without. I find that my specimens tend to sink, however, even if I use the reddish-brown hair from a summer Sika skin, which is a lot harder than red deer hair. I use the beetle on a floating line and handle it as a nymph.

OTHER BEETLES

In addition to the green and brown beetle there are many other species to be found washed down a stream, and I have noted several species in autopsies. Two widespread specimens I have copied and used successfully are the tiger beetle and the pinus longhorn. These are:

TIGER BEETLE   WET   HOOK: 10–12
Body: Grey speckled opossum fur spun on to thread. The body is slimmer than a brown beetle
Wing cases: Black and white speckled flank feather of paradise duck
Hackle: Two light turns of grizzle hackle.

PINUS BEETLE (LONGHORN)   WET   HOOK: 10
Body: Grey rabbit fur spun on thread. The body is long and slim, thickening towards the shoulder
Wing cases: Strip from grey duck wing secondaries
Hackle: Two turns of grey partridge

There is no end to the types of pattern that can be tied in this manner.

I think it should be recorded that there is a school of anglers who scorn most of the traditional beetle patterns, considering them to be made to catch fishermen rather than fish. They prefer to use other patterns, such as palmers, Hunt's Favourite etc. However, it cannot be denied that the beetle patterns do catch trout. But they are invariably poor floaters. I expect this is the reason for their unpopularity in some quarters.

The following two dressings should overcome this prejudice.

GREEN AND BROWN BEETLES (MORRIS'S) DRY HOOK: 12–14

GREEN:
Body: A good ginger palmer hackle
Wing cases: A bunch of green peacock herl tied in at the tail and brought over the top of the palmer and tied at the head. The herl is cemented with clear lacquer and flattened to form a wide top, suggesting the wing cases of the green beetle.

BROWN:

In this case the fly starts off as a palmer but a bronze breast feather from a cock pheasant is used to form the wing cases. The stem is left in to form a spine.

Both of these patterns are light and should prove wide acceptance. They are a compromise between the traditional beetle fly and the palmers so loved by many anglers when fishing the beetle rise.

BLACK BEETLE WET HOOK: 10–14
Body: Black wool
Hackle: Black
Wing cases: Pukeko wing

A simple and sometimes effective pattern.

BI-VISIBLE
(See PALMERS).

BLACK GNAT   WET AND DRY   HOOK: 8–14
Body: Ostrich herl dyed black
Wing: Starling quill
Hackle and whisks: Black cock or hen

   A gnat is the correct name for a mayfly or *ephemeroptera*, so it has always perplexed me that this is the only fly pattern actually called black. The Black Gnat is an old-world pattern and its original dressings are many. The dressings given here are the two most commonly found in use in New Zealand.

BLACK GNAT QUILL   WET AND DRY   HOOK: 12–16

   As above, except that a dark-coloured herl is used for the body.

   The first dressing appears to me to be of New Zealand origin, as I can find no overseas reference to a body of black herl, and we've yet to see a mayfly with a thick round body such as the fly to be found in New Zealand tackle shops. There can be no doubt that the success this pattern enjoys is due to its being taken by trout for a member of the blowfly clan, which as every angler will attest, abounds along back-country streams. I have often found these insects in a trout's stomach, with a resultant lack of interest in the fish's culinary prospects.

   With the Black Gnat Quill though, we have a definite copy of a mayfly and this fly can be used to good effect in a small size if small dark flies of the *Deleatidium* type are on the water.

BLACK GNAT SILVER   WET OR DRY   HOOK: 10–14
TWIST (DEANS)
Tail: Black
Body: Black ostrich herl ribbed with fine silver tinsel, either oval or round
Hackle: Black

   A Canterbury fly of unknown origin. It is used as a general pattern and no doubt is taken for a blowfly.

Wet and Dry Flies

BLACK HACKLE OR BLACK SPINNER — WET AND DRY — HOOK: 10–18

Tail: Black whisks
Body: Black floss
Hackle: Black cock

While it can and is often used as a wet fly this pattern is more commonly found tied as a dry. I have always thought of the Black Spinner as a very logical sort of fly. It so obviously imitates a spent spinner and depending on the size used must present a very passable silhouette, resembling several of the ephemerids. Used in the evening it is a good fly and I have used it with success on many occasions.

BLACK SPIDER — WET — HOOK: 12–14

Body: Brown silk waxed
Hackle: Glossy black feather from cock starling neck

This is the dressing recommended by the famous old Scots angler W. S. Stewart, who needs no introduction to students of angling literature. Readers will note the similarity of this border dressing with that of Captain Hamilton's Black Hackle used on the Manawatu nearly a century ago.

BLACK SPIDER — DRY — HOOK: 12–14 — GEORGE FERRIS

Of interest is the dressing given by Mr George Ferris, the well-known Canterbury angler and author, who dresses a fly with black hackle tied like a Palmer along the length of the hook and with a red tip on the body. Ferris claims that this fly is an excellent pattern when the balloon spider is drifting, and a better dry fly than any Dun when the fish are slow.

BLACK-WINGED DUN — DRY — HOOK: 12–16 — J. C. MOTTRAM

Tail: Two whisks of guinea fowl
Body: Black floss
Wings: Black cock points
Hackle: Grey

This pattern is J. C. Mottram's version of a representative copy of *Deleatidium lilli*.

BLUE BOTTLE   HOOK: 10–12   R. K. BRAGG
Tail: A short tuft of black squirrel
Body hackle: A good quality tapered black hackle is tied in point-first at the tail then wound up the body to the head, followed by turns of metallic blue lurex tinsel carefully wound through the hackle from tail to head.

Bragg claims that this is a very useful dry fly for backcountry rivers and is taken equally well by both rainbows and browns.

BLUE DUN   WET AND DRY   HOOK: 10–14
Wing: Starling
Body: Blue rabbit fur (eigther clipped from an ordinary skin or taken from the fur of a black rabbit)
Hackle and whisks: Blue dun, natural or dyed

I have often wondered if this fly, tied as a wet fly with its rather generous wings, is taken for one of the myriad blue butterflies that swarm in the summer grasses along the river's edge. Tied as a dry fly it is used to good effect when a hatch of blue duns (*Deleatidium lilli*) is on the water. This fly appears to be used more extensively in the South Island than it is in the North.

BLUE DUN QUILL

Perhaps the more effective pattern of the two is the one tied using a quill body. All other ingredients are the same as in the ordinary Blue Dun.

BLUE DUN (VARIATION) DRY HOOK: 14–16 R. K. BRAGG
Tail: Red cock hackle whisks
Body: Blue squirrel fur with a touch of brown olive seal's fur
Ribbing: Fine gold wire
Wings: Deer hair (natural grey) tied advanced
Hackle: Blue Andulusian

This pattern is used to copy one of the *Deleatidium* species and its inventor claims that it floats well.

BLUE DUN (VEINED WINGED) DRY HOOK: 14–16
R. K. BRAGG

Tail: Brown fox or squirrel
Body: Deer hair
Wings: Veined plastic tied in spent
Hackle: Rusty blue dun

Another of Bragg's patterns, this one represent the spent spinner of the *Deleatidium species*. Plastic wings are a controversial thing. They look very realistic and while some anglers praise them, others have nothing but scorn for their use. The reader may rest assured that if Bragg uses them, there can be no doubt about their effectiveness.

BLUE SPINNER (SPENT) DRY HOOK: 12–14

Tail: Blue dun whisks
Body: Rabbit's blue underfur
Wings: Grey hackle points tied spent
Hackle: Blue dun

I have come across this pattern on a couple of occasions. It is something of a misfit, as it has no parallel in nature, so far as I know. Yet trout will take it, so why should we worry. I expect the ventral silhouette is harder and more in keeping with a spinner than the softer appearance of the dorsal view.

BLUE UPRIGHT WET, BUT USUALLY DRY HOOK: 10–14

Another version of the Blue Dun is the Blue Upright. Authorities differ on the true dressing of this fly. Some say that only the brightest almost blue-black hackles should be used; another gives the dressing as medium-blue dun or dyed hackles. I think that the angler will find that New Zealand patterns are tied more in the latter vein. Certainly the patterns to be found in the shops would be described as being "Wingless Blue Dun Quill", and as that's a bit of a mouthful Blue Upright sounds more practical.

BRACKEN COCK   DRY   HOOK: 10–14   R. DICKINSON
Body: Bronze peacock herl
Hackle: Bronze breast feather of a cock pheasant stiffened with a bright ginger cock's hackle.

    The above dressing is given by R. Dickinson, who used the fly with success on the Tarawera River. It is an adapted version of an old North England pattern.

BRADSHAW'S FANCY   WET   HOOK: 8–14
Body: Bronze peacock herl
Hackle: Black crow neck
Tag: Bright crimson floss or wool with a couple of turns at the head, mingled with herl

    This is the original recipe for the fly, as used by an old Yorkshire angler after whom it was named. The New Zealand specimens I have seen and used have a grey hackle and a tag of red protruding over the eye as well as the proper one on the tail. The Bradshaw's Fancy is a good fly and is probably taken as a nymph of some sort. I have only seen it tied as a wet fly.

BRAGG'S CADDIS SEDGE WET HOOK: 10–14 R. K. BRAGG
Tail: Golden pheasant tippet
Body: Dark straw coloured chenille
Wing: Tuft of deer hair tied to flare upwards from hook

    This pattern is one of R. K. Bragg's range. While tied as a wet the deer hair wings help make the fly ride lightly and it is best fished on a floating line. It is probably taken as a drowned sedge, rather than a rising one, which indicates a dead drift.

BRER FOX   DRY   HOOK: 14–16   R. K. BRAGG
Tail: Brown fox
Wings: Brown fox fur tied advanced
Body: Blue-brown fur from the base of a brown fox tail
Hackle: Furnace

    This pattern was devised to copy the dun of one of the *ephemerids*, *Zephlebia versicolor*.

BRER RABBIT DRY   HOOK: 14–16   R. K. BRAGG
Tail: Red hairs from the base of a brown squirrel tail or red cock
Body: Body hair from whitetail deer spun between two threads, wound on and then cut close
Wings: Bunch of deer hair points (grey whitetail) tied advanced
Hackle: Blue dun. Rusty Andulusian preferred if obtainable

This fly comes under the Blue Dun group and is used to copy the dun of *Deleatidium lilli* when the local hatch of the insect has a pale appearance, compared with the darker version often found in some districts.

BROWN BEE   DRY   HOOK: 8–14   K. DRAPER
Tail: A good bunch of brown sika hair
Body: Brown velvet chenille
Wings: A mixture of kip tail and deer hair
Hackles: Two good ginger cock hackles tied fore and aft of the wings

A pattern of my own which kills well, both on rainbows and browns.

BUTCHER   WET   HOOK: 8–12
Wing: Blue mallard speculae
Body: Silver tinsel
Tail: Red ibis or dyed
Hackle: Black

In some English fly streams the Butcher is a banned fly, and to use it is considered *infra dig*. It is classed as a flashy lure and below the consideration of purists. It has been a popular fly, however, in New Zealand. I have seen some specimens of this fly tied long and slim; they are excellent flies for rainbow trout or estuarine browns.

BLOODY BUTCHER
The same as above except that a red hackle (dyed) is used.

CAPTAIN HAMILTON'S FLIES

For historical reasons I have included the dressings of the five flies used by Captain G. D. Hamilton nearly a century ago.

RED HACKLE — WET — HOOK: 8–12
Body: Yellow silk
Wing: Light brown mallard
Hackle and whisks: Natural red

Recommended for discoloured (even thick) water.

HARE S EAR — WET — HOOK: 8–12
Body: Hare's ear fur
Wing: Light woodcock
Hackle and whisks: Brown partridge

Recommended when the water is clear and low. (Readers will readily identify this pattern as a version of the March Brown).

BLACK HACKLE — WET — HOOK: 8–12
Body: Brown
Wing: Grouse
Hackle and whisks: Black

Recommended for clear low water.

BLACK SPIDER — WET — HOOK: 8–12
Body: Brown
Hackle and whisks: Black

Easily seen when the water is clear and low. A good fly to use as a tail fly when the trout are getting into high condition, or when they are shy due to bright sunshine.

Wet and Dry Flies

HARE'S EAR SPIDER   WET   HOOK: 8–12
Body: Hare's ear
Hackle and whisks: Brown partridge hackle tied with yellow silk

Very killing when the water is clear and low among high-conditioned and shy trout. Used as a tail fly this is perhaps the most reliable of the whole, particularly among large trout of two pounds and upwards.

Hamilton said of these five flies which had done him service around the world for more than fifty years: "These flies will do more execution than the largest variety with their endless list of names!"

He used three flies on a cast, or two if fishing a small stream, casting upriver in clear or tinted water. If the water was rather thick he recommended fishing downstream as the flies could be worked more slowly giving a trout a better chance to see them. I expect the good captain could give most of us a lesson today. Single-minded skills have been replaced with a proliferation of methods and theories and how many of us would proceed forth with only five patterns in our box?

CARDINAL   WET   HOOK: 10–14
Body: Red floss silk ribbed with gold wire
Wing: Swan or duck dyed red
Tail: As above
Hackle: Dyed red cock

This is a fly of which I have had no experience. However, it has been listed in several tackle dealers' catalogues for many years, so the pattern must have its adherents.

CICADA FLY   DRY   HOOK: 8–10   K. DRAPER

Using the idea of the molefly combined with the palmer I set out to attempt a copy of the cicada. This insect is an awkward shape with its wide head looking something like a back-tapered wedge. I gave the fly a good thick wind of ginger hackle up the hook and ribbed it with fine gold wire. A bunch of rolled hen pheasant wing was tied in at the shoulder to imitate a molefly. To get the brittle gauzy wings of the cicada I took four big points from bright sparkly hackles and tied them in on either side of the wing, keeping them a bit short. Then a good floating hackle was wound on the head. It floated well on a No. 10 hook and the trout took it. Its greatest success appeared to be in the Southland streams. A copy I sent to a southern correspondent was well taken by the big sea-run browns of that province.

COACHMAN   WET OR DRY   HOOK: 8–14
Body: Bronze peacock herl
Wing: White duck or swan
Hackle: Red or brown cock
Whisks: These are often omitted in the wet version or if included golden pheasant tippets are used. For the dry fly whisks of red cock are used to help support the fly on the water

The Coachman is many anglers' first choice as a dry fly. It combines the attributes of many other similar flies, but above all it has white wings. How many times in failing light have you watched the water, not quite sure where your fly is on the surface. You strike to a rise that wasn't to your fly and put down a fish, or else tighten too late. With the white wings of the Coachman drifting down like two beacons the uncertainty is greatly reduced. Besides, the Coachman is a handsome fly by any standards.

A good daytime version of the Coachman is a hackle pattern with the wing omitted. I have always called this the Hackle Coachman for lack of any other name. I was first introduced to this pattern by the late D. A. (Peter) Dawson, who was connected with the sports trade for many years. Peter tied a beautiful fly, but I can't recall ever seeing him tie a winged specimen, as he considered wings redundant. This Hackle Coachman was his sheet anchor, and I have used it with success on several rivers. It's a good basic fly and while Peter thought wings were redundant from a trout's-eye point of view, many will agree that they can be an advantage from the angler's point of view, especially if the drift is along and under a cover or background of dark vegetation.

COACHMAN (HAIRWING)   DRY   HOOK: 8–14
Tied as a hairwing the Coachman is a good heavy water fly. The dressing is as follows:
Tail: Bunch of deer hair
Body: Bronze herl
Wings: White calftail
Hackle: Double hackle of stiff red cock hackles

This is an American pattern that works well in New Zealand. It is particularly effective with the sea-run beauties of the South Island and the rainbows of the north. I have used this pattern often and find that on the heavy water of certain stretches of the Waikato it can be fished downstream on a short line and skittered on the surface. If it can be drifted and held over a spot where a trout has been marked, it will be only a matter of time before he will dart up to seize it. The rod tip has to be dropped immediately and the fish given several seconds to turn down before tightening. Actually this method of skittering a fly can be used to good effect with any good hackle fly such as a palmer or sedge.

CHURCHILL   DRY   HOOK: 12–16
Tail: Several short ginger whisks
Body: Straw-coloured silk
Wings: Starling
Hackle: Grey partridge

R. K. Bragg says this pattern was very popular in the Christchurch area about ten years ago, although its origin is obscure. The pattern, he says, was an extremely useful fly and had the appearance of a pale watery.

CHURCHILL   DRY   HOOK: 12–14   G. J. NILSEN
Tail: Mallard, dyed pale green
Body: Peacock eye stripped quill
Wing: Dark duck with strips of pale green mallard up the wings
Hackle: Dark furnace

This pattern was devised by Mr G. J. Nilsen of Motueka who, I am told, is a very knowledgeable angler, completely familiar with his district. I think it will be obvious that there is a connection between this pattern, the Canterbury version of the Kakahi Queen and the old King Country pattern of the Queen that has been around for years. I don't doubt but that Nilsen's pattern is a variation, based on observation of his local species of our old friend the dun of *Ameletopsis perscitus*.

CINNAMON SEDGE   WET OR DRY   HOOK: 10–14
Body: Cinnamon-coloured floss silk
Wing: Brown hen's wing
Hackle: Ginger cock
    An old-world pattern that kills well on most New Zealand streams.

COCH-Y-BONDHU   WET AND DRY   HOOK: 10–14
Body: Bronze peacock herl
Hackle: Dark furnace with black tips. (These hackles are fairly rare and while purists will insist on them I feel confident that any good dark furnace will do just as well. Where the proper Coch-y-bondhu is unobtainable we have little choice)

    This pattern is successful the world over and some anglers have claimed that with both the wet and dry patterns an angler needs no other fly. I think that this is an over-simplification, but there is a good measure of truth in the claim. The beauty is that it represents a good many insects which can be found at all times of the season. The name is a Welsh one, meaning red and black, and is named after a beetle with the same indigenous title. Beetles are beetles the world over and as I have said elsewhere the Coch-y-bondhu is a good fly to use when the brown or green beetles are swarming. The original pattern calls for a tag of several turns of gold tinsel around the shank of the hook. I seldom tie the fly with this adornment, considering it to be superfluous; indeed my friend Gordon Coulter, a very experienced angler, claims that a bright tag on the fly sometimes causes the trout to shy off. One South Island angler tells me that the Coch-y-bondhu has never done him any good.

    A large Coch-y-bondhu tied on a No. 8 hook and double-hackled is a favourite used by Southland and Otago anglers fishing for the large sea-run browns that enter the rivers in the late summer and autumn.

COCH-Y-BONDHU QUILL

As above except that a stripped peacock quill is used for the body. I'm not sure whether this is a New Zealand derivation, but suspect it is, as I haven't come across it anywhere else. I know several anglers who fish this pattern as a dry and with a fair measure of success. It is no doubt taken as an *ephemerid*.

COLEOPTERA

This is the scientific name given to the order commonly known as beetles. (See Beetles).

COWDUNG   WET OR DRY   HOOK: 10–14

Body: Yellowish-brown wool or fur mixture
Wing: Rail
Hackle: Ginger

I once met an angler who told me that this was the fly to use when the fish were on the brown beetle. He claimed it superseded any other fly. Since then I have met several others who hold similar claims for the fly. I myself have never used it, but I don't doubt that tied with a plumpish body it would, by the very nature of its colour, present a passable representation of the beetle.

CRANE FLY

This insect is often found along streams, as the larvae live in the damp ground along stream banks and in marshy areas. I do not think they could ever be classed as an important item on the trout's menu, but it is unlikely that one landing on the water through misadventure would ever be passed by, especially one so large as *Holorusia novae*, with its long legs spanning five inches and a wing span of two inches.

I once picked up an artificial crane fly in a sports shop years ago. For a long time I wasn't prepared to use it — it was such a work of art — but when I did decide to try it I lost it to the first fish to take it. Nylon casts were in their infancy in those days and the knots were

hardly ever to be relied upon. Alas, my office boy salary ruled out fine Spanish gut casts, so I had little choice. The pattern was:
Body: Brown raffia tied on a long-shanked No. 14 hook
Wings: Brown hackle tips tied in spent
Legs: Six pieces of fine gut knotted to form leg joints. Nylon or modern cast material serves the purpose admirably
Hackle: A minimum number of turns of long variant-type brown hackle

I think a vast improvement on this pattern is with the hackle tied in a parachute form.

It is as well to mention that the cranefly, or daddy-long-legs, is used on the lakes of Ireland as a natural bait. A long rod is used with a light silk line blown on the wind. As the boat drifts with the current the flies are dapped on the surface, and we are told of some great bags of trout being taken in this manner.

CRICKET FLY WET OR DRY HOOK: 8–12
Tail: Two short pieces of herl from a cock pheasant tail are tied in to represent the two claspers on the cricket's rear.
Body: Black chenille
Legs: Take two quills from a pukeko wing and cut the web off, leaving the short stubs along the spine. These are tied in with the body and bent to simulate the joints.
Wing cases: Pukeko wing tied in as a beetle
Hackle: Stiff dyed black hackle

Trout find crickets irresistible, as anyone who has fished where natural bait is permitted will tell you. I have also seen hundreds of trout rising in a Taupo bay to the countless thousands of small immature crickets that had been blown on to the lake. The above fly I have found to be accepted as an imitation.

DAD'S FAVOURITE WET OR DRY HOOK: 10–16
The origin of this particular pattern provides an interesting illustration of how some flies come by their names. Apparently an Invercargill sports shop imported some Dark Red Quill Spinners from England and on opening the consignment found that some of

the flies were not dressed in the correct manner, being too lightly coloured. Most of the local anglers wouldn't touch them, and for some time they sat in the trays unsold. The local butcher bought a couple to try out and found that they killed well. He bought more and was the only angler who thought highly of them. He would send his young boy off to the sports shop to buy him some before going out for an evening's fishing and the youngster would invariably greet the salesman with the request for some of "Dad's Favourites". That the fly eventually became a well-known pattern is now New Zealand angling history.

For many years I had always thought the Dad's Favourite a form of the Ginger Quill, and this contention was confirmed by several other anglers. Most commercial forms of the fly fall into this category, and the subject has often raised a difference of opinion. It was Robert Bragg of Christchurch who threw light on the situation, and no doubt others who agreed with me will be interested in his comments: "I would say that these two dry flies (Dad's Favourite and Ginger Quill) were not intended to be similar if tied correctly. Dad's Favourite should appear darker. The tail and hackle are tied from black and red Furnace, the body of stripped peacock with good contrast and a wing of waterhen."

This dressing can be compared with the Ginger Quill.

The Dad's Favourite is highly thought of, particularly in the Southland district, and its origin it seems, can be ascribed purely to accident.

DANIELSON'S DAMSEL FLY HOOK: 8–12 BERT DANIELSON
Body: Deer hair dyed black and tied as a detached body. It is secured to the hook then wound along most of its length with black thread.
Hackle: Black
Wings: Bunched pale deer hair tied spent

This pattern is the design of Christchurch angler Bert Danielson, and enjoys a good reputation on lakes and the margins of slower streams.

DEAN'S GRASSHOPPER   DRY   HOOK: 10–12

Body: Straw-coloured hackles wound palmerwise along the body and clipped to shape

Wings: Black (dyed) feather tied in penthouse fashion and cut in a halfmoon fashion then varnished

Hackle: Brown

This is a Canterbury pattern and is of unknown origin. It has been on the scene a good many years and would be used primarily in the summer.

DRAGONFLY QUILL   DRY   HOOK: No. 8

Body: A stripped spine from the primary of a bird. I used grey duck. The spine is tied to the hook and wound with blue or red floss. The last section of the quill is split to represent the claspers of the natural fly.

Wings: Four bright grizzle hackle points tied in, two of approximately equal length on each side and tied spent.

Hackle: Two long sparkly hackles are wound on. I have used a mixture of blue and ginger, but no doubt the sparkle is more important than the colour.

This pattern was given to me by Mr J. B. Thomasen, late of Taihape, and since the original was hackled with kiwi feather I have had to modify the dressing a little to allow a legal representation. Thomasen told me that this was a very successful pattern.

EARLY OLIVE DUN (NZ) DRY HOOK: 14–16 R. K. BRAGG

Tail: Barbs of yellowish-brown cock hackle

Body: Mixture of brown-olive seal fur and blue squirrel fur

Hackle: Grizzle hackle dyed yellowish-brown

Wings: Natural deer hair tied advanced

This fly was designed by its creator, R. K. Bragg, to copy the Ephemeridae family of Leptophlebiidae. (These insects are classed by Pendergrast & Cowley as Zephlebia). They are a small type of mayfly and extremely graceful in appearance. They are usually identified by their tails, which are longer than those of other duns.

ERMINE MOTH　　　　　　　**WET**　　　　　　**HOOK: 10–14**
Body: White rabbit belly fur ribbed with a strand of black wool
Hackle: Two grey partridge hackles
Tag: Orange

I have tied this pattern for a friend who used it with great success on the Waikato during the sedge rises. The orange tag possibly suggests a female laying eggs.

FANWING FLIES

This method of winging flies is attributed to the Americans. The flies appeared on the angling scene at the turn of the century. I have come across the odd specimen in anglers' boxes, but they are not in general use in this country. I don't doubt, however, that they would prove equally effective here as elsewhere. I have in my possession a coloured leaflet from one of New Zealand's early tackle firms showing two fanwing patterns, one the Grey Badger, the other a Stonefly. Both these flies had used partridge plumage for the wings which were tied spent rather than cocked at 45 degrees, which is the usual manner. This is intriguing, and it surprises me that these patterns never took on, as neither of them are to be found listed in present-day catalogues. Who knows, they may come into fashion some day. I have listed the dressing for these two flies in their alphabetical order.

The American manner of winging the flies consists of using a body feather from a mallard drake as a rule, although some rarer duck feathers are also favoured.

GOLD-RIBBED HARE'S EAR　　**WET OR DRY**　　**HOOK: 10–14**
Whisks: Several long guard hairs from a body skin
Body: Fur from a hare's mask with the blue roots clipped off with
　　several long fibres spun in at the head and picked out
Wing: Starling
Ribbing: Gold wire

This is a very old fly. It is given to us by Cotton, and possibly it was used for many generations before he recorded it in his treatise on fly fishing incorporated in later editions of the *Compleat Angler*. It is a pattern that has increased in popularity in New Zealand over the past few years, and we may find several variations of it used throughout the country. Some are local patterns but they all have one thing in common — the fur from a hare's mask is used. In some instances the body fur of the animal is used, and this is just as effective.

A true Hare's Ear uses no hackle; instead long fibres of the fur are wound in and picked out at the head with a dubbing needle. The chalk stream pattern is usually winged, although the wings are often dispensed with. Again I have seen some patterns tied with a couple of turns of good stiff hackle to assist the fly to float. It has been suggested that this fly is taken for a nymph that has reached the surface and is in the process of shucking and emerging as a dun.

GREEN CATERPILLAR   WET   HOOK: 10–14
Body: Green wool
Hackle: Grey wound palmerwise and clipped short

This pattern is not a common one, but I am told it will take trout well and is best fished on a floating line as a nymph.

GREENWELL'S GLORY (LIGHT AND DARK)
     WET OR DRY   HOOK: 10–16
Body: Primose floss silk
Wing: Inside of blackbird's wing
Hackle: Furnace (coch-y-bondhu)

If I had been born 100 years ago I might have been tempted to have become a cleric. They seemed to spend a lot of time fishing, and Canon William Greenwell of Durham was no exception. He was nearly 100 years old when he died, and the fly which he devised was first tried on the river Tweed in 1854.

The Greenwell's Glory has been used with great success the world over, and would be one of the most popular wet and dry flies in New Zealand. The above dressing is the way Greenwell first devised the fly.

Today it is hard enough to get furnace capes to dress these flies, let alone coch-y-bondhu. Courtney-Williams says that in New

Zealand a bright red tag is favoured, but I have never come across this or been able to locate an angler who had. The Greenwell is well received in this country as a dry fly and when oiled the body takes on an olive hue. The trout will take it under many conditions, and its popularity is aptly expressed by the late F. E. Thornton, who when editor of the *Fishing and Shooting Gazette* said in the August 1950 edition:

"Our favourite fly is the Greenwell's Glory and we kill a lot of fish on it. Like you: 1. We know of no fly it represents in New Zealand. 2. For that reason we know not when to use it, but on the other hand we rarely use any other fly, so why worry!"

This philosophical outlook can be applied to many other patterns, and indeed many overseas authorities are not prepared to say what the Greenwell represents in their own area. Thornton's outlook is truthful and refreshingly frank.

A version of the Greenwell that appears to be a New Zealand pattern in as much as I cannot find any overseas reference to it is the Greenwell's Dark, which uses a dark green floss body. This along with the regular Greenwell's is ribbed with fine gold wire. In both patterns the use of whisks is employed.

Yet another version I have been asked to tie is the Greenwell's Quill, which involves the use of a body of stripped peacock quill. This version, an excellent one, can be used to represent several species of Ephemeridae.

GREENWELL (STUDHOLME'S) DRY HOOK: No. 14
R. K. BRAGG

Tail: Stiffest barbs from dark furnace cock spade hackle
Body: Yellow seal's fur
Hackle: A bright cock furnace hackle wound palmerwise down the body and secured with a gold wire over-rib

Designed by Bragg at the request of Mr H. M. Studholme, this fly has proved to be an excellent knockabout hackle fly. Its inventor says that the fly is also taken well as an imitation of the *Deleatidium myzobranchia*.

GREY BADGER   DRY   HOOK: 10–14
Tail: Ginger whisks
Body: Grey Floss
Wings: Grey partridge breast feathers tied fan wing spent.
Hackle: Grey

This pattern is apparently an English one and used to be sold in this country about thirty or more years ago. It is probably intended as a copy of one of the large British mayflies and doesn't seem to have survived. I include the dressing as anglers are more dry fly-conscious these days, and the pattern may prove to be successful in some districts.

GROUSE SERIES   WET   HOOK: 8–14
Wing: Grouse tail
Tippet: Golden pheasant
Bodies and Hackles:
  Green with ginger hackle (Grouse and Green)
  Orange with red hackle (Grouse and Orange)
  Purple with black hackle (Grouse and Purple)

These old Scottish wet flies were once very popular throughout New Zealand and I remember having success with a Grouse and Orange found in a tin of flies given me by an old angler. Some were so old they had little eyes made of twisted gut whipped to snell hooks.

The Grouse and Purple is a good evening fly, probably taken as a sedge. It is favoured in the South Island. Grouse feathers are becoming harder to procure, which may pronounce the death knell for these flies in this part of the world.

HACKLE FLIES

This term is applied generally to dry flies, although it belongs equally as much to wet flies. It means that a fly is tied without wings. Many of the dry fly patterns can be tied in this manner and they kill very effectively. There are some schools of thought which claim that wings on a dry fly are quite superfluous, and I am inclined to agree with them, having used hackle flies with success on many occasions. However, wings do help an angler to observe his fly's progress in uncertain light. And if the wings are white, buff or a pale colour, it is much easier to determine whether a rise is to your fly or another natural fly.

Where wet flies are concerned most of the spiders and partridge flies of English (North Country) origin are tied in this manner.

HAIRWING FLIES WET OR DRY

As the name implies this term is used to describe any pattern of fly that uses a wing made of hair. The hair can be from a great variety of animals, perhaps the most popular being deer hair or calf tail. Basically they are of American origin, but there are many anglers in New Zealand who have used them for years.

Dry flies tied with hair wings are good fish catchers, and a popular style of fly is the famous Wulff series, the designs of the American angler and author Mr Lee Wulff. There are many anglers in New Zealand who have been using these patterns with success.

HARDY'S FAVOURITE WET OR DRY HOOK: 10–14
J. J. HARDY

Body: Peacock herl ribbed with red floss
Wings: Dark brown turkey
Hackle: Dark partridge
Whisks: Brown mallard

This fly was designed by the late J. J. Hardy of the famed tackle firm. It is a good fly for use in New Zealand and is to be found in the flybook of nearly every stream angler. Fished downstream and across it is probably taken for a nymph pattern, as the soft partridge hackles lie close to the hook in the water. I doubt that anyone would be game to claim that it represented anything in particular, and like the March Brown, wet, it could representa large may fly nymph, a drowned moth, a sedge nymph or an adult sedge. It is a good general fly and in the evening it can be fished dry if it is double-hackled and strengthened with the addition of a good cock hackle wound in as well. The dressing above is the true one, although you will seldom find it in New Zealand. The variation, while quite dissimilar in some

respects, is often tied in the United Kingdom. This is the one you will usually find in use here:
Body: Peacock herl ribbed with red floss
Wings: Hen pheasant
Tippets: 3–4 golden pheasant tippets
Hackle: Grey partridge

HECKAM PECKAM　　　WET OR DRY　　　HOOK 10–14
Body: Red wool or seal's fur ribbed with silver
Wings: White-tipped speculae feathers from a mallard drake
Hackle: Red cock
Tail: Golden pheasant tippets

Here is an old Aberdeenshire pattern attributed to one William Murdoch. I doubt that it now sells as well in New Zealand as it once did, as it seemed to be in nearly every old flybox that you came across. I am told that the fly is still very popular in Canterbury. Twenty years ago my editor, David Elworthy, used it with great success in South Canterbury streams.

HOFLAND'S FANCY　　　WET OR DRY　　　HOOK: 10–16
Body: Reddish-brown tying silk
Wings: Woodcock or hen pheasant
Hackle and whisks: Red cock

According to Hofland himself this fly is dressed as above. The pattern usually found sold in New Zealand, however, has a magenta body which does not come under the heading of reddish-brown. But it is a favoured pattern, and a fly used by many anglers in the Manawatu-Wairarapa-Hawke's Bay area early in the season. It is used there mainly as a wet, but is also well favoured by some dry fly anglers. This pattern also kills well in the South Island.

Thus we are using a fly in New Zealand which is not really a Hofland at all. Yet it kills possibly just as well, perhaps even better. It should be known by another name, but no doubt it never will be. It seems that the magenta-bodied version was sent out here by Farlows of England. G. G. Kelly tells me that he argued this dressing error with them over forty years ago, but it made no difference.

HOME BREW   DRY   HOOK: 10–14
Body: Bronze peacock herl
Tail: Golden pheasant tippets
Hackle: To suit in either ginger, red, grizzle or black

"Streamline", writing in the *New Zealand Fishing and Shooting Gazette* of November 1956, gave the above dressing for the home fly-tier. While they closely resemble several other patterns they nevertheless do take trout very well when tied on a size 12 or 14 hook, or even smaller. They are recommended as dry flies and I can personally attest to the effectiveness of two of the patterns, although I have never got around to trying the pattern with the grizzle hackle.

The only feature I do not care for in these patterns is the tippet whisks. I never care for them on a dry fly as they lack the stiffness of good hackle fibres and many times a fly will sit back on its tail. Good stiff whisks help it to float better.

HUNT'S FAVOURITE   DRY   HOOK: 10–14   A. H. HUNT
Tail: Red cock
Body: Copper-coloured peacock herl
Wings: Starling or duck
Hackle: Red cock

The late A. H. Hunt began tying flies at Monowai, Southland, in 1931 and it was not long before his work was in popular demand. This fly is very similar to a leadwing Coachman but to many southerners the "Hunt" is as well known as the Red Tipped Governor in the north. Readers of Hobbs will no doubt have been as puzzled as I was on reading of a "Double Hunt". Bragg tells me that when a double was ordered it simply meant a fly dressed with a double amount of hackle or double split wings.

The fly is highly regarded by many South Island anglers as a beetle fly, especially when the brown beetle fall is in the river.

HUTTON'S BLACK BEETLE   DRY   HOOK: 10–14
                                                                 MAJOR SUTTON
Body: Blue floss tied thinly
Wing: Peacock sword tied flat on top of body
Black cock: Tied in after wing has been secured

HUTTON'S BROWN BEETLE DRY HOOK: 10–14
MAJOR SUTTON

Body: Light brown floss
Wing: Peacock sword tied flat on top of body
Hackle: Red hackle, tied in after wing has been secured

Two popular Canterbury patterns. The late W. Satterthwaite of the Wairarapa, who fished the South Island for many years, told me that he considered the Black to be one of the best back-country lake dry flies that he knew. Both patterns are the creation of the late Major Sutton, a well known South Island angler.

INVICTA WET OR DRY HOOK: 10–14

Body: Seal's fur dyed yellow
Rib: Gold twist or thread
Body hackle: Red cock tied palmerwise
Shoulder hackle: Blue jay tied over the red
Wings: Hen pheasant tail feather
Tail: Golden pheasant crest

This is the dressing of the Invicta as designed by James Ogden of Cheltenham, England. It was tied as a sea trout pattern or a lake fly, but it was used with some success as a sedge fly in the north of England.

Above is the correct dressing, but I haven't yet come across one in New Zealand tied with the body hackle. To illustrate how mutations come into being the following story is of interest. A tackle dealer came to me with an Invicta, a much simplified version of the above dressing. I had no jay wing on hand, as it is hardly ever used on any of our patterns, so I took some darkly-banded grey mallard flanks and dyed them blue. Everyone was pleased with the outcome, and the fly became established. The dealer soon had anglers coming from many miles away for the pattern, and soon one of them wanted it tied as a dry. Now the Invicta is strictly speaking a wet, but after bolstering the soft blue hackle with a bright ginger hackle to give it lift, this fly was also taken by the brown trout of that district. Technically speaking it was now no longer an Invicta, and to complicate matters further, I dropped on request the dyed mallard and replaced it with cock hackle dyed blue, still backed with the ginger. And this is how a certain tackle shop still sells the "Invicta".

JESSIE SERIES

JESSIE No. 1   WET AND DRY   HOOK: 10–14
Tail: Black whisks
Body: Brown floss
Wing: Speckled turkey
Hackle: Black

JESSIE No. 2   WET AND DRY   HOOK: 10–14
Tail: Black whisks
Body: Bronze peacock herl
Wings: Speckled turkey
Hackle: Black

JESSIE No. 3   WET AND DRY   HOOK: 10–14
Tail: Claret whisks
Body: Bronze peacock herl
Wing: Speckled turkey
Hackle: Claret
   (This one is often called the Jessie Claret)

JESSIE No. 4
Tail: Black whisks
Body: Purple with gold rib
Wing: Speckled turkey
Hackle: Black

In his book *The Flies in My Hat*, G. G. Kelly tells how the postmaster at Kakahi in the King Country designed this series many years ago. They were named after a small girl, Jessie Freeman, who died only a few years ago, in her eighth decade. I am not certain that the dressings given above are absolutely correct, as there has been some uncertainty as to which was what. This is the problem with numbering a series. The Jessies aren't as popular as they once were, except perhaps Nos. 2 and 3. The plump herl bodies have assured their continued success.

KAKAHI QUEEN WET AND DRY HOOK: 10–14
BASIL HUMPHRIES

Body: Stripped peacock herl quill
Wing: Mallard duck fronted with mallard breast dyed yellow
Hackle: Golden furnace (Greenwell's)
Whisks: As hackle

This fly was devised at the same time as the Twilight Beauty by Mr Basil Humphries, postmaster at Kakahi. G. G. Kelly tells me that it was invented to copy a fly that was common on the Whakapapa river although he could not be certain about the exact species. I have discussed this with other anglers, and it appears to be the general consensus that the fly copies one of the Ephemeridae, *Ameletopsis percitus*, a mayfly distributed over most of the country. Christchurch angler Peter Laing says: "One of the best copies of any of our New Zealand mayflies is the Kakahi Queen. This fly when hatching is usually found in good numbers and if the Queen is used, much better sport can be had."

R. K. Bragg confirms that the fly Laing refers to is indeed *Ameletopsis percitus* and the following is a dressing that is in vogue in the Canterbury district:

DRY HOOK: 14–16

Tail: Bronze Mallard fibres
Body: Peacock quill built up with a humped thorax
Wings: Waterhen with strip of pale green (lime) in front of wings
Hackle: Badger

Bragg says that the above variation is still tied in Christchurch although he prefers the original Humphries dressing. The first dressing appears to be in vogue in Southland, where the same insect is to be found. A similar dressing is to be found under the heading of Churchill (Nilsen's).

LACE MOTH DRY HOOK: 12–16

The Lace Moth is the local name given for a leaf hopper which abounds in some districts, especially Taranaki, the King Country and the Bay of Plenty. I have seen a King Country stream boiling with rising trout as myriads of the little lace moths covered the water, and at such times the trout were very difficult to catch.

A pattern used a lot in the Bay of Plenty area, and the dressing favoured by the late J. Morris, is as follows:
Body: A dubbing of rabbit fur, not too large, as the lace moth has a relatively small body in comparison with its wing span
Wing: A breast feather is taken from a mallard drake, preferably from the edge of the chestnut breast. This is given a thin coating of lacquer and the delta-shaped wing cut from it. The whole feather is then laid on top of the body and tied in at the stem.
Hackle: A couple of turns usually ginger, of good bright hackle are used, but I have also seen grizzle used, which is more in keeping with the natural coloration of the insect.

Another pattern tied by Walter Willis of Te Kuiti is made up as follows:
Body: Fawn ostrich herl
Wing: Paradise duck breast feather from the male bird, cut to shape as in the above pattern.
Hackle: Nil
Hook: 12–14

R. Dickinson in *Rising Fish* claimed that representative lace moth copies never did him any good, but that when the fly was on the water the following pattern did the trick for him:
Body: Grey or blue-grey fur or wool (mole being ideal)
Wing: Nil
Hackle: One small grey partridge and one ginger hackle
Hook: 12 or 13

LOVE'S LURE   DRY   HOOK: 10–14
Body: Bronze peacock
Wing: Green peacock sword
Hackle: Black cock

This is a South Island pattern and a very effective representation of a beetle. I have come across it in the North Island on a few occasions, and it is highly thought of by those who recommend it.

MAGGOT CADDIS   WET   HOOK: 10–14
Tail: Dark red game
Body: White silk thread ribbed with black glace thread
Hackle: Dark red game

    R. K. Bragg first came across this pattern twenty years ago when it was sent to him to tie by Mr G. J. Nilsen of Motueka. Nilsen claimed that the fly was a pattern of good repute in the Nelson area, and a good general fly.

MALLARD SERIES   WET   HOOK: 8–14

    Many of these excellent patterns have fallen out of favour over the years, but for some time they represented the backbone of the wet fly angler's range of flies. They are all old-world patterns. Some of the patterns were tied on large hooks and they killed well in the Taupo and Rotorua districts. Tied with long swept-back wings they made excellent lures and today one pattern is still very popular. It is the Mallard and Claret, a pattern that must have killed tons of New Zealand trout over the years. It is especially favoured as a night fly. Its dressing as tied in New Zealand differs a little from the original form.

MALLARD AND CLARET   WET   HOOK: 8–14
Body: Claret seal's fur or chenille ribbed with gold
Wing: Bronze mallard
Tail: Tippets
Hackle: Claret

MALLARD AND BLUE   WET   HOOK: 8–14
Body: Light blue seal's fur or wool, silver ribbed
Wing: Bronze mallard
Tail: Tippets
Hackle: Dyed blue cock

MALLARD AND GREEN   WET   HOOK: 8–14
Body: Green seal's fur or wool, silver ribbed
Wing: Bronze mallard
Tail: Tippets
Hackle: Dyed green

Wet and Dry Flies

MALLARD AND BLACK   WET   HOOK: 8–14
Body: Black seal's fur or wool, silver ribbed
Wing: Bronze mallard
Tail: Tippets
Hackle: Black

MALLARD AND RED   WET   HOOK 8–14
Body: Red seal's fur or wool, gold ribbed
Wing: Bronze mallard
Tail: Tippets
Hackle: Red, natural

MALLARD AND ORANGE   WET   HOOK: 8–14
Body: Orange seal's fur or wool, gold ribbed
Wing: Bronze mallard
Tail: Tippets
Hackle: Dyed orange

MALLARD AND SILVER   WET   HOOK: 8–14
Body: Flat silver tinsel with a silver rib
Wing: Bronze mallard
Tail: Tippets
Hackle: Black

MALLARD AND GOLD   WET   HOOK: 8–14
Body: Flat gold tinsel with gold rib
Wing: Bronze mallard
Tail: Tippets
Hackle: Ginger cock

MALLARD AND YELLOW   WET   HOOK: 8–14
Body: Yellow seal's fur or wool with gold rib
Wing: Bronze mallard
Tail: Tippets
Hackle: Ginger

MAMMOTH
See THOMPSON'S MOTH

MARCH BROWN   DRY OR WET   HOOK: 8–14
Body: Hare's fur spun on yellow thread
Hackle: Brown partridge
Wing: Hen pheasant wing secondaries
Tail: Partridge tail (several fibres)

Here is a fly used the whole world over wherever trout are to be found. Its variations are endless, as are its possibilities. It can be tied to represent a dun, a sedge, a moth, a nymph, or even in the larger sizes a salmon fly or lure. It is a killing pattern and I often consider it owes much of its success to the fact that it is of sober natural colours, without any flashiness. Whatever variations we may consider, the above is the basic dressing of all March Browns.

Tied as a dry fly most anglers will find that it floats better if the partridge hackle is reinforced with a good stiff ginger cock's hackle. It is often tied with double partridge hackles when used as a dry but these are inclined to become clogged with oil and constitute a soggy mess. This style of dressing is quite good for sedge fishing when it doesn't seem to matter much if your fly doesn't float too well. Rabbit fur is often used for the body dubbing, and in the case of the March Brown female a turn of yellow wool or silk is incorporated in the tail end of the body. This is commonly supposed to represent the female insect in the act of exuding eggs.

Now that brings us to a very tickly question. What is a March Brown in the natural state? I have put this to many anglers and have yet to receive a satisfactory reply. The nearest I have ever come to it is a mayfly, a member, I think, of the Deleatidium group. I have often seen this fly on the water from May through to October. It is very much like a March Brown artificial with a mottled brown wing and a brown body. I have seen it in the central North Island district on several occasions when I have been dogging a stream for waterfowl, and I particularly recall one August afternoon when fishing the Waitahanui below the bridge when a large hatch of these duns came down the water. The small fry were rising all over the stream but my interest and that of the other dozen or so anglers fishing that stretch of water was concentrated on the big fresh-run winter trout that were hugging the bottom of the stream. The latest I have seen this particular fly on the water is in October, although it could occur at other times. Taking the fly as it is dressed in New Zealand, one is forced to the general conclusion that the pattern more closely resembles the sedges than any other order of insects, excepting perhaps the stonefly. But its ultimate success usually lies in the manner in which the artificial fly is dressed and then presented.

MARCH BROWN CLARET   WET   HOOK: 8–14
Tail: Partridge whisks
Body: Black seal's fur
Wing: Hen pheasant
Hackle: Claret

This pattern is sometimes referred to as the Irish March Brown. While not common, it is used occasionally.

MARCH BROWN PURPLE   WET   HOOK: 8–14
Tail: Partridge whisks
Body: Purple floss with silver rib
Wing: Hen pheasant
Hackle: Purple

This pattern is often referred to as the Scotch March Brown. It is a good pattern and one I used a great deal several years back. It fishes well cast upstream.

MAYFLIES
See EPHEMEROPTERS

MINSON'S FANCY (SPIDER VARIANT)   DRY   HOOK: 12–14
I. J. D. MINSON

Tail: Long bright red cock
Body: Dark brown thread
Hackle: Dark to medium brown cock hackle wound palmerwise along the body from tail to head

This fly tied for Mr I. J. D. Minson, a Christchurch angler, is used to good effect on the Halswell river and streams near to Christchurch, says R. K. Bragg, and recommends the Minson as an excellent fly when the mayfly *Deleatidium sepia* is on the water. Apparently the original dressing was attributed by Minson to a Dunedin angler, the late John McConey, a sub-editor for the New Zealand *Listener*.

MOLEFLY   DRY   HOOK: 8–14

Body hackle: Red cock tied palmer fashion and ribbed with gold wire
Wings: Hen pheasant
Hackle: A good floating hackle of red cock
Whisks: Red cock

Here is an old English pattern that is used to very good effect in this country. It was originally tied to represent a mayfly, although Courtney-Williams tells us that the fly is widely used in France, where it is considered to be an excellent sedge pattern.

This is also the opinion of many New Zealand anglers, who agree that it kills very well when trout are rising to the sedge. The difference here, however, might lie in the method of winging. The old English style is tied with the wing cocked high and sloping forward. I have seen this tie only on a couple of occasions, and they were probably imported flies. The customary manner of tying uses a good rolled wing sloping back, which gives it a sedgelike appearance.

Many anglers have also found the Molefly to be an excellent day fly for dry fly fishing, especially when fishing blind. The fly floats well and is usually tied on a No. 10 or 12 hook — and even as large as a No. 8 when fishing rough streams or for large searun browns. The Molefly is a particularly good pattern on back-country streams when the trout are feeding on cicadas.

The fly is often tied with ginger hackles and I sometimes think that this is an improvement for the daytime version, as it is possible to import more sparkle than with red hackles.

MONTREAL   WET   HOOK: 10–14
Body: Bright red floss ribbed with gold
Tag: A bunch of red floss
Wings: Hen pheasant
Hackle: Red cock

Here is a Canadian pattern that will take rainbows very well. I have no experience of it on brown trout, and it is not a widely-used fly. I have fished it in Hawke's Bay with success.

MOTTRAM'S MAYFLY DUN   DRY   HOOK: 12
Tail: 3 barbs of guinea fowl
Body: Grey floss
Wings: Pair of grey cock hackle points
Hackle: Pale ginger (almost yellow)

MOTTRAM'S MAYFLY SPINNER   DRY   HOOK: 12
Tail: Black cock barbs
Body: Dark chestnut floss
Wings: Cut white hackle tied spent
Hackle: Two turns of dark red cock

These two patterns were devised by J. C. Mottram, an early English angler. These two dressings, along with many others first given by G. B. Hobbs in an appendix of his excellent book on angling in New Zealand, *Fisherman's Country*, published by Geoffrey Bles Ltd., London in 1955. Readers may note a slight difference in the above dressings from the originals. The improved dressings are those of R. K. Bragg and the deviations are but slight. The insect they represent, *Ichthybotus hudsoni*, is the largest of our known Ephemeridae. A very similar species, *Ichthybotus bicolour* is so similar that they can be treated by the angler as the one type.

MURRAY'S FAVOURITE   WET OR DRY   HOOK: 10–16
Tail: Bronze mallard
Body: Peacock eye quill
Wings: Speckled hen
Hackle: Natural black

This pattern is a Southland one and originally a wet, but it has proved to be very effective as a dry. R. K. Bragg tells me that he believes it was first dressed with a hackle of grey partridge.

NIMMO'S KILLER   DRY OR WET   HOOK: 10–16   BERT NIMMO
Body: In two sections; the rear half red floss, the forward portion black ribbed with fine silver wire
Hackle: Furnace
Tail: Tippets

This fly was the creation of the late Bert Nimmo of Wellington, well known in angling circles for his artistry with the fly rod. This fly can best be described as a fancy fly, and was used by Nimmo with great success on the Hutt river. The Nimmo is used all over the country with success and while it is usually used as a dry fly it will kill quite well as a wet.

OLIVE DUN   DRY   HOOK: 12–16
Tail: Dyed olive whisks
Body: Olive seal's fur or wool
Wings: Starling or light duck
Hackle: Dyed olive cock. (Some prefer the olive dyed on a ginger feather, giving the hackle a golden hue)

This pattern is claimed by Mr Walter Gibb to be the ideal companion to Welham's Red Spinner, both patterns being used on Southland's Mataura. He was not able to say exactly what species of mayfly it was taken for, but was of the opinion it was one of the *Deleatidium* group.

ORANGE SPINNER   DRY   HOOK: 10–14
Whisks: Ginger cock
Body: Bright orange wool ribbed with gold wire
Hackle: Sparkly ginger cock

Here is an effective dry fly for summery days. What it represents I can't really say, but the trout do like it. Tony Orman tells me of his success with it on the Maraetotara and Tukituki. A similar type of dressing given by Courtney-Williams is claimed to be effective in the United Kingdom when the ichneumon fly is on the water, and there could be a New Zealand parallel, as this insect (the soldier fly as we commonly call it), is to be found all over the country. It is at its peak in the summer months.

Wet and Dry Flies 133

ORANGE WOODCOCK   **WET**   **HOOK: 10–14**
Body: Orange wool with fine silver rib
Hackle: Sparse turn of woodcock breast feather

This spider pattern is one of the old English border patterns and kills very well on the New Zealand scene. It has cropped up often enough to warrant its inclusion here. It is fished upstream and serves well if cast as a nymph on a floating line.

PALMER FLIES

Palmer is a term used to describe a fly that is hackled along the whole length of its body, lending itself to several variations of underlying body colours and hackle overlaps. The Americans originated a form of this tie known as a Bi-visible, incorporating a two-coloured fly, the front hackle usually white to give the fly visibility. Palmers are usually fished dry but as they are a very old pattern they must have been used as wets many years ago. I have seen an old reference to palmer flies where they were described as being a good imitation of a caterpillar. They would have to be tied with very short hackles as no one in his right senses would describe a modern palmer fly as looking anything like a caterpillar. These flies float nearly as well as thistledown.

The palmer is usually considered to be a good fly to use on a hot bright day. There are in fact several patterns of flies that are really winged palmers. Two that come readily to mind are the Molefly and Wickham's Fancy.

PALMER BLACK   **DRY**   **HOOK: 10–14**
Body: Black floss
Hackle: Black cock
Rib: Silver

The Black Palmer is almost as highly regarded by some as the Red Palmer. The fly illustrated was tied by the late J. Morris, who considered the pattern to be an important one for dry fly anglers. The dressing for this fly was given by Walton who would, of course, have used it as a wet fly.

PALMER RED　　　　　　　DRY　　　　　　　HOOK: 10–14
Body: Red floss
Hackle: Red cock hackle tied palmerwise and ribbed with gold wire
Tag: Bunch of red wool

In this pattern you will often find the red tag omitted and replaced by whisks of the same material as the hackle. The Red Palmer is liked by all dry fly men and many consider it to be the best fly for fishing blind. Some consider it a good pattern to use when the brown and green beetles are on the water. A Christchurch angler, Mr Peter Laing, tells me he considers it superior to all the standard beetle patterns. He prefers a size 14, claiming it will float all day long.

PARACHUTE FLIES

This is a special method of tying a dry fly and as it is time-consuming parachute flies are not often found in the shops. They are sometimes tied on special hooks that have a projection standing up from the shoulder of the hook for the purpose of winding the hackle around. The hackle sits over the fly like the ribs of an umbrella. This method of tying represents a spinner and can look very like the real thing.

A method of tying parachute flies on standard hooks is to use the lower stem of a hackle as a pedestal. The end is tied in and cemented to the top of the hook, then a loop bent in the spine and tied in again. The whole base is given a good cementing, then the hackle is wound around the upright loop, tied in, cut off, and a drop of cement placed on the centre. When this has set, the top of the pedestal loop is cut off.

I have tied these flies to help clients take over-cautious trout from clear streams, and they have worked where other flies have been ignored. They float very low in the water, just as a spent spinner does.

Mr W. Broad of Wellington gave me a small pattern he has used on the Wainuiomata with success. He used a small bunch of white calf tail for the pedestal, leaving a small tuft projecting to act as a marker. His body was of dubbed rabbit and the hackle was honey dun.

These flies have never become a marketable proposition, but for the angler who ties his own they are to be recommended.

PARADISE OR PARRY SERIES

When I was a youngster and beginning to make my own flies, I invented, as I thought, a new pattern. Based on a Teal and Red, I tied the same pattern using the flank feather of a paradise duck. It has a teal-like barring, although much darker, and the bands are not so distinct. Anyway it caught trout and I thought myself rather clever.

Some years later I was to find that it had all been done before. Not as well known as other patterns, they are based on the body dressings of the Teal and Mallard series and are equally as effective. They are of course, wet flies, but like most of the wet fly patterns they are losing out to the nymph fishing rage that has swept the country. The paradise duck feathers are very useful for fly dressing and any amateur is advised to obtain a skin if he can. Much of the plumage, wings included, is very useful.

PARTRIDGE AND HARE'S EAR   DRY   HOOK: 10–16
Whisks: Bright ginger cock
Hackle: Brown speckled partridge feather
Body: Fur from a hare's mask dubbed lightly
Rib: Fine silver wire

This old United Kingdom pattern was one of the late J. Morris's favourites. As a floater it can be improved with a few judicious turns of stiff grizzle hackle wound among the partridge.

PARTRIDGE AND ORANGE   WET   HOOK: 14–16
Body: Fine orange tying silk whipped with fine gold wire
Hackle: Two turns of small brown partridge

Brian T. O'Rourke, writing in the *Fishing & Shooting Gazette* in 1955, gives us this pattern, which he says he used with success on that difficult Canterbury stream, the South Branch. It is an old North Country Spider pattern and O'Rourke says that he fished it upstream on very light gut so that it rode on the surface, which suggests to me a fair measure of line and rod tip control. He added that if the fish do not come to it, but appear to be rising, thoroughly moisten the fly and fish it as a nymph.

PEPPER WINGED DUN DRY HOOK: No. 14 J. C. MOTTRAM
Whisks: Guinea fowl
Body: Grey floss
Wings: Light ginger points tied in upright
Hackle: White

PEPPER WINGED SPINNER DRY HOOK: No. 14
J. C. MOTTRAM
Whisks: Two long fine black barbs
Body: Dark chestnut floss silk
Wings: White cock hackle cut
Hackle: Nil

These two patterns are J. C. Mottram's tie to represent the *Coloburiscus humeralis*. They were designed over seventy years ago so far as I am able to ascertain, but have never taken on. The Spinner looks good, especially if a few turns of hackle are added. However, Mrs Alice Harmer, who ties for Tisdalls of Christchurch, says that she was been asked to tie them on very few occasions and in each case apparently no repeat orders were forthcoming. Perhaps they may find favour one day, but for historical reasons at least they are worthy of a place here.

PETER ROSS WET HOOK: 8–14
Tail: Tippets
Body: Tail half silver tinsel, front half red seal's fur ribbed with silver wire
Wing: Teal
Hackle: Black

This fly is named after an old Scots angler. Along with many other excellent loch patterns, the Peter Ross was brought to New Zealand where it soon became a favourite. But it is not to be found in the tackle shops as it once was.

PEVERIL-OF-THE-PEAK   WET OR DRY   HOOK: 8–14
Body: Bronze peacock herl
Wing: Blue white-tipped speculae of a mallard
Hackle: Red cock
Whisks: Red cock

Who Peveril was, or where the peak was situated, I do not know and neither can I find out. I am unable to find this fly in any overseas listings so perhaps it is a New Zealand pattern. John Wells tells me he thinks it is an old Derbyshire pattern. Whatever its origin it is an excellent fly for our conditions and probably represents a beetle of some sort. What stands the Peveril apart is its wing and while many of us question the need of a wing on many flies, it is an advantage on this particular pattern. The white lips stand out clearly as it floats over dark water, and greatly aid the angler with indifferent vision. It is also used as a wet, but I think it is as a dry fly that it is most greatly valued.

PHEASANT TAIL   DRY   HOOK: 10–16
Body: Fibres from a cock pheasant tail ribbed with gold wire
Hackle: Golden dun cock
Tail: Golden dun

This fly kills very well on New Zealand waters. Some anglers I have met have the highest praise of it. The pattern is helped with the addition of a fine wire rib which helps keep the body together. A trout's teeth play havoc with the brittle pheasant tail fibres.

POMAHAKA (RED AND BLACK) WET OR DRY HOOK: 10–16
Body: Black or red floss, ribbed with gold wire
Wing: Blackbird
Hackle: Black
Whisks: Black

These flies are named after the Pomahaka River in the South Island, a tributary of the Clutha. They are fished both wet and dry, although they are more favoured as dry flies, probably representing spinners of the mayfly order.

They are very similar to the Waipahis, which were developed on a neighbouring river.

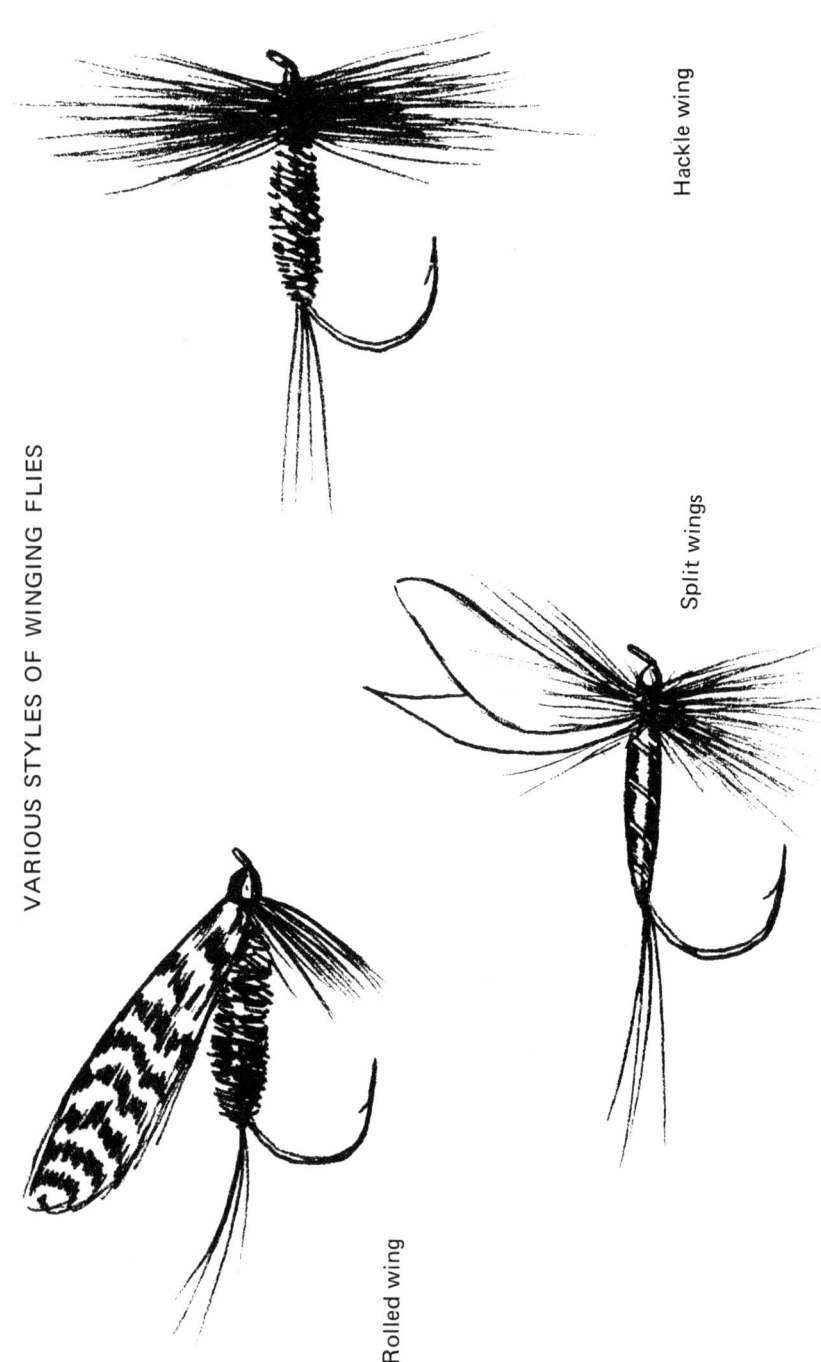

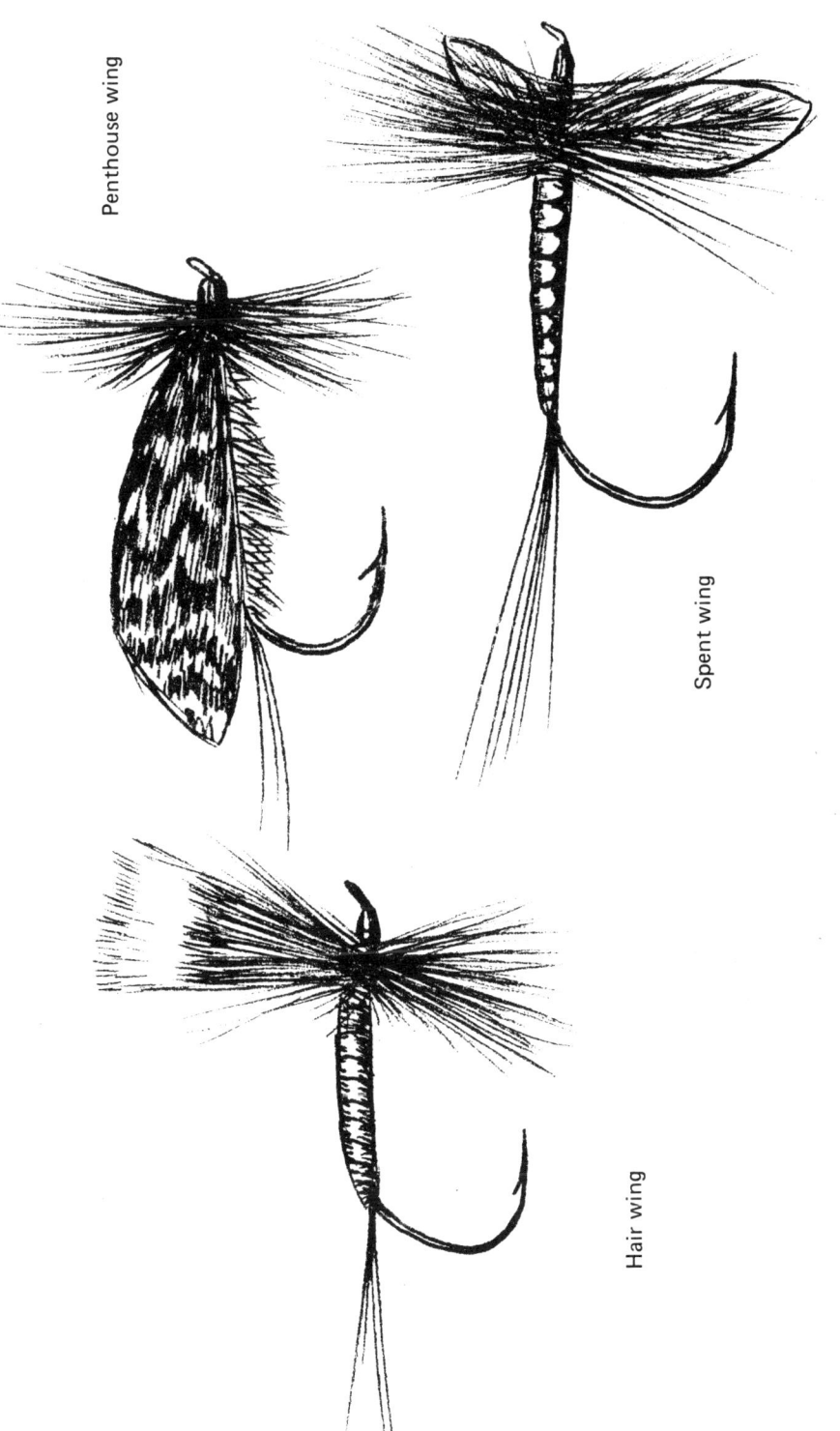

POPE'S NONDESCRIPT DRY HOOK: 10–14
Body: Light green floss ribbed with gold
Wing: Starling
Hackle: Bright red cock
Whisks: Red cock

This a popular New Zealand dry fly and has many adherents, especially in the south. For many years I used a version of this fly tied purely as a hackled spinner omitting the wings, and it killed well on several North Island streams. I found that the more sparsely hackled version which rode rather low in the water was taken more readily by the trout. I have seen this version tied on extra large hooks, even as big as a No. 6, and used on rough water streams, where it was quite effective.

PRIEST DRY OR WET HOOK: 10–14
Body: Flat silver ribbed with silver thread
Tail: Red ibis
Hackle: Badger

This is a pattern not often come across, but it does crop up occasionally. I myself feel that this pattern would fish better as a wet fly.

PYE'S SEDGE DRY HOOK: 10–12 ALAN PYE
Body: Ostrich herl dyed yellow (an ochre shade is the one desired)
Wings: Black shag feather tied penthouse
Hackle: Dark ginger

Mr Alan Pye of Huka Lodge, on the Waikato River, just a few miles from Taupo, has long enjoyed a reputation as an angler of note. Those who have seen him fish the dry fly have described him as being without peer.

The Waikato is well known for its sedge rises, although hydro-electric developments have by now ruined this fishery. A large type of sedge (HYDROPSYCHE), with very dark wings used to be taken by trout to the exclusion of all else, so Pye set about making a copy of it. This fly turned the tables and is now used in many parts of the country with the same success that it enjoys on the Waikato.

QUILL FLY

This term is applied to those flies having a body made from quill. In the case of such flies as Ginger Quill and Kakahi Queen the body is made from the fibre of one of the eye filaments of a peacock tail feather. The herl is rubbed off and the thin strip wound on. These give an excellent imitation of the body of many of the mayflies. However, other quills may be used, and strips from the feathers of some birds give bodies of interesting formations in varying natural colours.

RED FOX   DRY   HOOK: 14–16
Tail: Lightest red cock
Body: Blue squirrel fur mixed with hare's ear
Ribbing: Fine flat gold
Hackle: Light red with two turns with a blue Andulusian hackle wound in front

This is an R. K. Bragg variation of the Blue Dun group representing the *Deleatidium lilli* species. It will appeal to those anglers who prefer a straight hackle fly to a winged version.

RED HACKLE   WET   HOOK: 10–14
Hackle: Red cock
Body: Red wool

Angling historians tell us that this fly was in use nearly 2000 years ago when the Greek Aelian (A.D. 170-230) recorded that the Macedonians used a lure made of red wool wrapped around a hook and two waxen-coloured feathers from a cock's wattles attached to it. It is a simple dressing and kills as well today as it did long ago in Balkan mountain streams.

RED QUILL OR RED QUILL GNAT   DRY   HOOK: 10–18
Body: Stripped peacock herl (eye)
Wings: Pale starling
Hackle and whiskers: Red cock

Halford described this fly as the sheet anchor of the dry fly fisherman when on a strange river. To a certain degree the same could be said of it in this country, especially on those streams that enjoy a good hatch of ephemerids. Like many other anglers, I think of it as a more lifelike version of the Red Spinner, as there can be no argument that the quill body looks much more natural than a floss one. Many believe that the patterns one sees in shops are a little on the large size and that this fly, like so many other dry flies, will kill much better if fished in smaller sizes, say 16 or 18 — certainly no larger than 14. You find these patterns in the shops tied on size 10 and 12, a little on the large size if you compare the size of one of these flies with the natural.

A variation of the Red Quill was given in *New Zealand Outdoor*, October 1956, when a contributor using the pen-name "Mac" described a hairwing version of the pattern he had used with success. The fly was dressed with wings of grey hair tied in at a 45-degree angle.

RED QUILL HACKLE   DRY   HOOK: 12–18
Tail: Dark red whisks
Body: Peacock eyed quill
Hackle: Dark red cock

This is a simplified dressing of the Red Quill and is a favourite of the wingless dry fly school.

RED SPINNER   WET AND DRY   HOOK: 10–16
Body: Red silk with gold thread ribbing
Wings: Starling
Hackler and whisks: Red cock

The Red Spinner is well known the world over and has found its place in New Zealand. In its wet form it is a good general purpose fly, but it is as a dry fly that the Red Spinner excels. There would hardly be a dry fly angler who hasn't used this fly at some time. You will often hear anglers speaking of a natural form of the Red Spinner, but few agree just what it is. However, it would appear that the fly is one of the *Deleatidium* species of the mayfly group. The Mataura midge is the spinner or imago of one of these species, and as a spent spinner they drift down that river in countless thousands.

Mr Walter Gibb, who often fished the Mataura, showed me a fly tied by the late Lester Welham to imitate this spinner. The following is the correct tie.

Wet and Dry Flies

RED SPINNER (WELHAM'S)　　　DRY　　　HOOK: 16 or 18
Whisks: Several barbs of dark blue (dyed) cock hackle
Body: Tail half-red, ribbed with black tying thread. Fore half black
Hackle: Red cock
Wings: A thin section of pale hen pheasant wing tied in spent and clipped

Apparently this pattern of Welham's was so successful that a wholesale firm had the fly copied and distributed under the name of Red Spinner. Gibb tells me that the dun of the Mataura spinner is successfully matched by the Olive Dun, while G. Ferris in *Fly Fishing in New Zealand* tells of using the Blue Dun.

However all exponents of the Mataura are emphatic that whatever the pattern used, size is critical and only the smallest of flies will be accepted by the trout.

RED SPINNER (DARK QUILL)　　　DRY　　　HOOK: 14–18
Tail: Dark red whisks
Body: Dark peacock quill
Wing: Dark starling or blackbird
Hackle: Dark red

This is a very popular pattern. I have often seen it tied with the wings spent and it is an excellent fly in the smaller sizes.

RED SPINNER (LYSAGHT)　　　DRY　　　HOOK: 10–16

Tied as a Red Spinner except that partridge tail, tied bunched, is used for the wings.

RED TAG　　　WET AND DRY　　　HOOK: 10–16
Body: Green peacock herl
Hackle: Bright red cock
Tag: Red wool

Here is a very handy fly which has all that is required of a good killing pattern. The red tag served me very well once in the Manawatu district. In this case I used a small No. 16 fly and fished it as a nymph. Before using it I picked out most of the tag, leaving a few strands only, to suggest, rightly or wrongly, a wounded insect. Perhaps it might have worked as well without my going to the trouble, but these were educated browns I was after and the thick tag looked a little too ostentatious.

RED-TIPPED GOVERNOR WET OR DRY HOOK: 8–14
Body: Bronze peacock herl
Wing: Hen pheasant wing quill
Hackle: Red (natural)
Tip: Red floss

Here is everyone's favourite. I'll wager there is hardly an angler of experience who hasn't used one at some time or other. Fished wet or dry it is a good reliable pattern and I recall the afternoon when as a bare-legged boy I took thirteen trout out of one run on the Governor. It is an excellent pattern used as a dry fly, probably suggesting a beetle. The Governor is sometimes tied with a yellow or orange tip, the original fly being an old English pattern. It would seem, however, that the version so popular in New Zealand is an American derivation of the original.

RELISH DRY HOOK: 10–14
Body: Dark claret seal's fur
Hackle: Dark red cock's hackle wound palmerwise and ribbed with gold wire

A general purpose fly of South Island origin.

ROYAL COACHMAN WET AND DRY HOOK: 10–14

Any angler beginning wet fly fishing for the first time will always buy a Royal Coachman to put among his other "pretty-looking flies". This pattern is an American version of the ordinary Coachman and I doubt whether for all its fine looks it kills any better. That it does take trout there can be no denying, and I have used it myself often in the past. I used to use it on my top dropper but I think it is a better pattern when used as a dry. But as I have said it does nothing that the ordinary Coachman will not do.

If you tie your own flies you will agree with me that it hardly seems necessary to put a red cummerbund on its body. This is a flytier's view and the same could be said of many other patterns. The Royal Coachman is the largest-selling fly in the United States, and while there is a demand and a market for it here in New Zealand, it is my experience that New Zealand anglers prefer their Coachman straight.

SETH GREEN WET AND DRY HOOK: 10–14
Body: Bright green floss with a yellow silk ribbing
Wing: Grey of wild duck wing
Hackle: Red cock
Tail: A few strands of teal or mallard flank

This fly bears a close resemblance to Pope's Nondescript and it will kill just as well. I have come across this pattern several times and for that reason feel it worthy of inclusion.

SHELDON'S FANCY DRY HOOK: 8–12 G. N. SHELDON
Tail: A bunch of dark red cock hackles
Body: Dark wine-coloured silk
Wings: Hen pheasant tied spent
Hackle: Dark red cock

This pattern was devised by a Christchurch angler, G. N. Sheldon, as a copy of the small lake damsel fly. He considers it an effective pattern to use on lakes in hot glassy conditions, the procedure being to fish from the bank to cruising trout.

SHOO FLY DRY HOOK: 10–14
Tail: Whisks of scarlet dyed cock
Body: Bronze peacock herl
Wings: Veined plastic
Hackle: Rhode Island Red

R. K. Bragg tells me that this fly appeared on the Canterbury scene several years ago but its origin is unknown. It is also tied as a variation with a yellow fluorescent body. Both patterns are highly regarded on the back-country lakes.

SHRIMP FLIES

GOLD SHRIMP   WET   HOOK: 8–12

Tail: Short strands of pheasant tail (tips)
Body: Gold tinsel
Backing: Pheasant tail fibres tied over as a beetle wing case, the ends being whipped back to form legs of sorts.

SILVER SHRIMP   WET   HOOK: 8–12

Tail: Short strands of bronze peacock herl
Body: Silver tinsel
Backing: Bronze peacock herl tied as for the gold shrimp.

HORNER SHRIMP   WET   HOOK: 8–12

Tail: Short brown bucktail
Body: Built up with wool then covered with heavy silver tinsel
Backing: Brown bucktail
Hackle: Pale olive

The three patterns above are variations of an old English tie made very popular by Hardy Bros. R. K. Bragg gave me these dressings which have proved popular in the South Island. I have used a slim dressing of this type for smelting trout. This style of fly is sometimes known as a minnow fly and for this purpose is better tied on a long shank hook. For a shrimp style of tie a standard limerick hook is best. A pattern I have been asked to tie is as follows:

Body: A thin dubbing of rabbit fur with a soft ginger hackle wound palmerwise
Tail and top: A back of deer hair tied in beetlewise with two long hairs left protruding as feelers

SILVER SEDGE   DRY   HOOK: 12–14

Hackle: Ginger, wound palmerwise
Wings: Pale starling or duck tied penthouse

I have seen hatches of this fly on rivers well before dark but only odd specimens. The pattern given above will kill well on many occasions, even when the natural is not in evidence.

Wet and Dry Flies 147

SNELLED FLIES

Before eyed hooks came into being the gut cast was whipped to the shank of the hook before the fly was dressed. The gut was usually of short length and looped so that a further length of cast could be added by slipping another loop through. The end of the hook was flattened to prevent the whipping from slipping off. Needless to say snelled hooks went out with the Ark, but an exporting friend of mine recently had an enquiry from overseas for snelled flies. Today they are a relic of the past, but any angler who has any in his possession should have them preserved as they are of historic value. Another version of snelled hooks is to be found in some salmon flies, where the eye was formed by whipping a small loop of twisted gut to the hook.

SOLDIER PALMER

So far as I am able to ascertain the dressing for the Soldier Palmer is identical to that of a Red Palmer. The title Soldier appears to stem from the fact that this pattern is used in the United Kingdom when a reddish beetle known as the "soldier" is on the water.

SPIDER FLIES

There are countless species of spider and a great many of them are to be found near, on, or even in, water. The spider fly is an old favourite and there are many variations of the pattern to be found. Any reader who has come across that grand old classic of angling, *The Practical Angler* by W. C. Stuart, will know what great store the old Northern English and Scots anglers placed in their spiders. The patterns are all tied in much the same way, with a small body of silk or wool, no whisks and a soft hackle that reaches back about halfway down the body. A lot of these patterns were to be found in the fly books of New Zealand anglers half a century ago, although they are now almost ignored by the more sophisticated anglers of this modern age.

The spider patterns go hand in hand with long willowy rods and braided silk lines, but they will kill just as effectively today with more modern equipment. For curiosity I tied a couple of spiders recently and tried them out one evening. There was a good rise on, and although the trout were small they took the spiders perfectly. I fished them on a floating line and they came down just under the surface. The two patterns I used were a black spider tied with black wool and a small black hackle from the neck of a pukeko, and a brighter version with an orange body and a hackle of grey partridge. Like many old patterns that have been forgotten the spider, tied on small-hooks, is a style of wet fly that could be used with profit on many occasions. Perhaps they are taken for rising nymphs rather than spiders, especially when they swing against the current, the soft hackles being swept along the body.

STANLEY'S FAVOURITE (BEE FLY)   DRY   HOOK: 10–12
JOHN STANLEY

Tail: Golden pheasant tippets
Body: Yellow chenille (a variation uses fluorescent yellow)
Hackle: Medium brown cock
Wings: A pair of white-tipped, blue-black feathers taken from a starling skin

This pattern, sometimes known as the "Bee", is a good backcountry lake pattern according to R. K. Bragg, who first dressed this fly to the instruction of Mr John Stanley of Christchurch.

STONE FLY

The stone fly is to be found the world over and is represented in this country by several species. While its larva is often found in a trout's stomach the adult fly is not always so evident. They are weak fliers and almost bumble along. While I have come across the larva often I have seen the adult fly on but few occasions. The flies hide among the grasses and streamside bushes and seldom fly except after dark.

One dressing I have come across is a fairly good representation of a stone fly. Dressed on a long shank hook it resembled a lure. It was dressed as follows:

Hook: 10–12
Body: Brown floss ribbed with gold
Wing: Bronze mallard tied in a semi-penthouse position and sloping well back over the tail, the ends rounded
Whisks: Long red cock
Hackle: A couple of turns of red hen

Another specimen of fly I have come across is a dry. G. G. Kelly tells me it was one of Farlows' (England) patterns. This is its dressing:
Hook: 10–12
Body: Grey floss
Wing: Speckled partridge tied fan-wing and spent
Hackle: Redcock
Whisks: Several fibres from a cock pheasant tail

The next pattern is similar to some used overseas, but is the one favoured in the Canterbury district. R. K. Bragg kindly supplied the following dressing:
Tail: Two strands from a partridge tail
Body: Blue fur ribbed with yellow silk, several close turns at tail end
Wings: Soft side of hen pheasant wing quills, tied in long
Hackle: Medium blue dun

SUMMER DUN (MORRIS) DRY HOOK: 10–16 J. MORRIS
Hackle: Pale glassy badger
Body: Ostrich herl dyed golden olive tied with yellow thread
Rib: Fine silver wire
Whisks: Badger

This pattern is the creation of the late J. Morris. In some of his written notes he says that it was a most useful general-purpose fly for Bay of Plenty rivers. The pattern he tied is lightly dressed, but the hackles are of a fine glassy appearance, and when held to the light catch and reflect the flashes of sunlight such as might be expected with the gauzy wings of a spinner, rather than a Dun. I don't doubt, however, that Morris had a very good reason for calling the fly a Dun, and the very reason that this old angler thought so highly of it makes it worthy of consideration by all dry fly men.

SUMMER FLY   DRY   HOOK: 10–14   K. DRAPER
Tail: About a dozen red body hairs from a summer sika deer pelt
Body: Short thick butt of bronze herl
Wing: Buff hen pheasant wing
Hackle: Ginger palmer hackle with a good double hackle at head

This is a dry fly of my own design. It incorporates the features of several successful flies; an excellent floater, it is visible, and it really does catch trout. It does present a problem in that every small trout in the stream appears to be attracted to it, but on the law of averages it takes its share of big trout as well. I have called it my Summer Fly as this is the time of the year when it does so well, especially during very low water. The buff-coloured wings show up well under all conditions. I find size 14 to be the smallest practicable size, but no doubt it would go well on some streams as large as size 10. I have not tried it on slow clear waters, as it was designed for the rougher water we encounter in so many of our central North Island streams.

TEAL SERIES   WET   HOOK: 8–14

These flies were in demand a generation or two back and several old anglers' tackle boxes I have come across have invariably held some of the teal patterns. Teal feathers have become very expensive and no doubt many New Zealand anglers found that there were other patterns which killed as well. The teals have lost a little in popularity today but they served very well for many years and no doubt if given the chance would still do the same. I have used the Teal and Red and Teal and Orange to good effect in the past, but it is some time since I had one on my cast. As I have pointed out elsewhere the New Zealand paradise duck has a flank feather that makes a fairly good teal substitute although it is a little heavier in the black tones and is not so predominantly barred. The flank of a mallard drake also makes a substitute, but in this case the feather has a much more silvery-grey effect. The following are five popular dressings.

TEAL AND RED
Body: Red floss or wool, with silver ribbing
Wing: Teal flank
Hackle: Red cock
Tail: Tippets

TEAL AND ORANGE:
Body: Orange floss or wool, with gold ribbing
Wing: Teal flank
Hackle: Ginger cock
Tail: Tippets

TEAL AND GREEN
Body: Green floss or wool, with silver ribbing
Wing: Teal flank
Hackle: Black cock
Tail: Tippets

TEAL AND BLACK
Body: Black floss or wool, with silver ribbing
Wing: Teal flank
Hackle: Black
Tail: Tippets

TEAL AND SILVER
Body: Silver tinsel
Wing: Teal flank
Hackle: Blue
Tail: Tippets

TEMUKA WET HOOK: 8–12
Body: Bronze peacock herl
Wing: Grey mallard flank
Hackle: Claret

Mr Noel Thomas of the Temuka Sports Centre tells me this pattern was very popular forty to fifty years ago. Who designed it is not known, but it was probably well taken when the trout were feeding on the brown beetle.

THOMPSON'S MOTH WET HOOK: 10–14 G. M. THOMPSON
Body: Cream or white chenille
Wing: Hen pheasant
Hackle: Mottled brown partridge

This is a popular South Island pattern that was designed by a member of parliament, the late Hon. G. M. Thompson. It is an effective pattern after dark when used as a sedge. I believe one river on which it is very effective is the Clutha.

TONGA   DRY   HOOK: 10–12   J. FROST
Tail: Golden pheasant tippets
Body: Peacock herl ribbed with red floss
Wings: Tied spent from the lesser coverts of starling wing
Hackle: Red cock mixed with one brown partridge hackle

This pattern was the invention of J. Frost, who ran a tackle shop at Turangi for many years. The fly was once considered essential for back-country fishing in Canterbury. It was reputed to be an excellent killer when the fish were rising to the red damselfly.

TUPS INDISPENSABLE DRY HOOK: 12–16 R. S. AUSTIN
Body: Two sections, the tail yellow floss with a thorax of the pink tup
Hackle and whisks: Honey dun cock hackles

This is an English pattern, the creation of a Mr R. S. Austin of Tiverton. Austin kept the ingredients of his fly a secret and it was eventually Skues who was given permission to make public the secret ingredients of the Austin fly. Anglers were surprised to learn that the main item used in the dubbing ingredients was the stained wool from around a ram's pizzle. The wool was washed and then mixed with some cream-coloured seal's fur, lemon spaniel's fur and a pinch of crimson seal's fur.

Now why such a mixture should constitute a telling recipe I wouldn't even hazard a guess—some of the old English patterns smack of witchcraft. Today sheeps' wool dyed pink is used. I have no great experience of the Tup myself but I do know several anglers who claim it is a very killing fly. It is also used, perhaps more frequently in this country, as a nymph. One style of dressing I have come across was tied as a parachute spinner, the body consisting of two portions, the rear half yellow floss and the forward section pink floss.

TURKEY SEDGE (DARK)   DRY   HOOK: 8–10
Body: Hare fur with gold wire rib
Wing: Dark turkey tail varnished, doubled over and clipped to shape
Hackle: Dark red

This pattern is very killing in the Waikato River, where I use it to copy the large dark sedge that is to be found there.

TURKEY SEDGE (SPECKLED)   DRY   HOOK: 10–14
Body: Hare fur with gold wire rib
Wing: Speckled brown turkey wing secondary, varnished doubled, over and clipped to shape
Hackle: Ginger

Another pattern designed to copy the more common but smaller Waikato sedge. This caddis fly is distributed over much of the country, and has dark blotches on its wings, being about $\frac{5}{8}$ in. long, not including the antennae. The above pattern kills well in most districts at dusk and after. Anglers to whom I have sent copies have reported success in both islands.

TWILIGHT BEAUTY   DRY AND WET   HOOK: 10–16
                                                     BASIL HUMPHREY
Tail: Ginger
Body: Black floss
Wing: Blackbird primary (or native grey duck wing)
Hackle: Ginger cock

Here is a good, reliable New Zealand fly that is used all over the country. It is used a great deal as a wet and when dressed in this way I have long considered that it is taken for a sedge. Dressed as a dry there can be no doubt that it is taken as a mayfly and the name Twilight Beauty is often given by many anglers to the spinner of *Coloburiscus humeralis*, a fairly common fly to be seen on many streams through much of the summer.

It hovers in clouds over the pools in the late evening and the female is to be found on the water dipping along as she drops her eggs. The Twilight will take trout when they are up to the spinner.

The wet is a very effective fly after dark. Greg Kelly in *The Flies In My Hat* tells of the origin of the Twilight Beauty. It was the design of Mr Basil Humphrey, postmaster at Kakahi in the King Country. Since the fly was intended to be a copy of a mayfly there can be little doubt that it was intended to represent *Coloburiscus humeralis*. There is evidence, however, that the fly may also be taken when the spinners of *Oniscigaster distans*, *Ichthybotus hudsoni* and *Ichthybotus bicolor* are on the water.

TWILIGHT BEAUTY (LAING'S)   DRY   HOOK: No. 14 2X
                                          PETER LAING
Body: Black floss ribbed with fine gold
Wings: Blue dun points tied spent
Hackle and whisks: Ginger cock

This pattern is the result of close observation by Mr Peter Laing of Christchurch. The fly is much more natural-looking than the ordinary Twilight and is tied as a spent wing. The effect is a very gauzy fly and of course the natural always has that quality about it.

TWILIGHT BEAUTY (HUMPED VARIATION)   DRY
                                               HOOK: 12–16

A favourite of R. K. Bragg, this pattern is dressed in the normal manner except that the body is built up around the thorax, forming a lump directly behind the hackle. This is not the orthodox type of tie, but is much in favour in the South Island.

TWILIGHT BEAUTY (LIGHT)   DRY   HOOK: 12–16
Tail: Ginger whisks
Body: Light fawn floss
Wings: Duck
Hackle: Ginger

A Taranaki version of the popular Twilight, this dressing is popular in the Stratford area of that province. The pattern suggests the ventral aspects of several of the ephemerids, and I am surprised that this pattern is not more widely known.

UMBER SPINNER   DRY   HOOK: 12–14   K. DRAPER
Body: Umber brown floss or wool
Hackle and whisks: Umber (either dyed or from a Rhode Island/ Black Orpington cross)
Wings: Grey points — optional

   I tie this pattern to represent the female of what I call the Umber Spinner (*Colorburiscus humeralis*). This large spinner is fairly widely distributed during most of the summer. A good fly that I can recommend when the trout are taking the spent spinners. I have also used it with success before the actual spent was to be found on the water. It will also serve very well when the imago of both *Ichthybotus* and *Oniscigaster* are on the water.

WAIPAHI (RED AND BLACK) WET AND DRY HOOK: 10–14
Body: Black or red floss
Wing: Blackbird primary
Hackle and whisk: Black cock

   These are two Southland patterns which have their origins on the Waipahi which, together with the Pomahaka, forms part of the Clutha watershed. As pointed out in the Pomahaka patterns, there is little difference in these patterns apart from the use of tinsel ribbing in the latter case. They are both used as wet and dry flies.

WEST COAST BEETLE   DRY OR WET   HOOK: 8–14
Tail: Medium brown hackle points
Body: Rust-coloured wool tied plump
Wing cases: Green peacock sword, tied forward as usual except that the ends are not cut off, the tips left sticking up to produce a sort of wing
Hackle: Medium brown

   This pattern is the West Coast version of the Manuka Beetle.

WHITE MOTH   WET AND DRY   HOOK: 8–14
DRY
Body: Rabbit belly ribbed with fine silver tinsel
Wing: White duck
Hackle: White cock
WET
Body: White floss
Wing: White duck
Hackle: White hen

The White Moth is a pattern that is more favoured in the South than the North Island. It used to be very popular, but seems to have been replaced in the North at least, if not elsewhere, by the more natural-looking sedge ties. The dry is well taken by trout in the evening and I recall dapping one in a small stream that was heavily grassed along the banks. I chose the fly because of its visibility, which I think is its main attraction so far as anglers are concerned. On this evening though, the small trout of that stream went mad over it as I let it drift along short runs under my very rod tip.

WICKHAM'S FANCY   WET AND DRY   HOOK: 10–14
Body: Gold flat tinsel
Body hackle: Ginger cock ribbed over with gold wire
Shoulder hackle: Ginger cock
Wings: Starling

An English pattern of the chalk stream, the Wickham is widely used in New Zealand, both as a wet and a dry fly, although the original and correct tie is as a dry. It is a good pattern for bright days as indeed are most flies incorporating a palmer tie. I have found the Wickham to be an excellent fly for using as a sedge tied on a No. 10 or, if fishing in heavy water, ever a No. 8 hook.

WILLIE'S WHOPPUMS   DRY   HOOK: No. 6
Body: Bright green floss with gold rib
Hackle: Stiff cock's hackle, either natural red or ginger
Tail: 3–4 strands of pheasant tail

In the *New Zealand Outdoor* of January 1960, R. J. Brown gives this dressing of a style of fly that he had found to be an excellent floater on rough mountain streams. These outsize flies are tied on

No. 6 hooks and need to be well hackled. As they are used in rough water there can be no doubt but that trout take them for any insect that has inadvertently fallen in the water, if they are to make the most of nature's bounty they must seize the hapless creature before the swift current carries it out of their pool. This pattern, like the Seth Green, reminds me of the Pope's Nondescript.

WOODCOCK SERIES   WET   HOOK: 12–16

This series, along with the teal, mallard and grouse was in much use a generation ago. In some districts they have survived well, although they are to be found winged as often as not with hen pheasant, which bears a very close resemblance to woodcock. But the latter has an almost imperceptible pinkish tinge to it. The trout don't seem to discern the difference. They are normally fished wet.

WOODCOCK AND GREEN
Body: Green floss or wool, silver wire rib
Wing: Woodcock
Hackle: Ginger but sometimes dyed green
Tail: Tippets

WOODCOCK AND RED
Body: Red wool or floss, silver rib
Wing: Woodcock
Hackle: Red
Tail: Tippets

WOODCOCK AND YELLOW (WOODCOCK AND GREENWELLS)
Body: Yellow floss with gold rib
Wing: Woodcock
Hackle: Furnace
Tail: Tippets

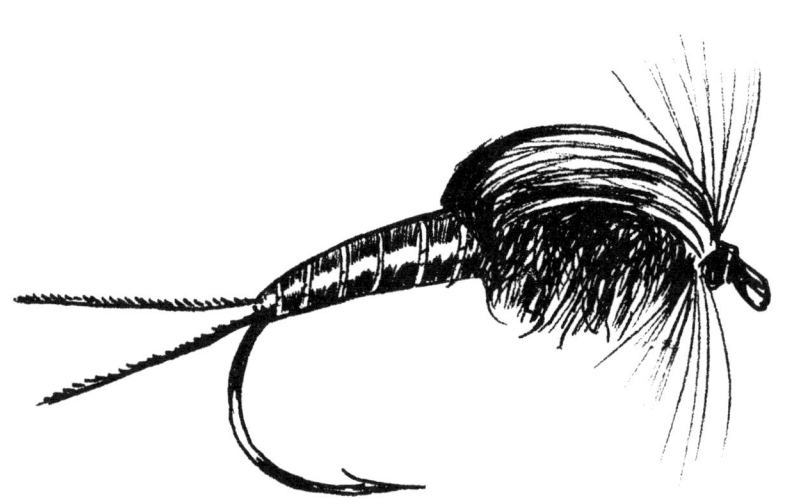

4

NYMPHS

Nymph fishing has taken the angling world by storm and New Zealand is no exception. I think that Skues could be called the father of modern nymph fishing, although man has used nymphs since the earliest days of fly fishing. It is not very far removed from upstream wet fly fishing.

Most of the old wet flies could be classed as a form of nymph, especially those lightly dressed soft hackle patterns, and we all know how well a March Brown fishes after half its wing and dressing have been worn or chewed off. I often fish a nymph pattern on my deep-sinking line and I know of several summer fishing spots where this form of fishing is especially successful. A nymph may be loosely described as the larva of any insect that lives in a stream or lake, and this covers a wide variety of species with differing habits.

It was Skues who set about bringing the art of nymph fishing to its purest form. He was concerned with the rising nymph of the mayfly when it leaves the stones and weed beds on its hazardous trip to the surface where it splits its thorax and 'the dun emerges, riding down on the surface of the stream.

Trout feeding on these nymphs appear to be rising, when in fact they are feeding below the surface, the rings being caused by their swirl as they take the insect near the top of the water. Fish feeding at this time can be very selective indeed, just as selective as when they are taking a hatch of duns or a fall of spinners. This is an art and calls for a certain measure of skill in correct presentation, although the trout might not be so critical on a swift stream as they would be on a flat-surfaced clear stream.

In this type of fishing a floating line is used and the cast greased along most of its length. This is a matter of individual taste, some leaving only a few inches ungreased while others a foot or so. Often the fly is taken unseen by the angler, especially if the light is in the wrong quarter. A stoppage of the line or a twitch of the cast may be the only indication. Sometimes you will see the line move off upstream. If the light is favourable you may see the fish take, or notice the flash of its side as it turns to take the artificial nymph.

All of these signs demand an immediate response by the angler and the hook should be set as soon as possible. Not a cast-breaking strike but a firm tightening of the rod. The fish will set the hook as soon as he feels the bite. A delay will often result in only a pricked fish, but there are many occasions when the fish are kind enough to hook themselves and the first thing one knows of their presence is when they are firmly on. On the other hand, I have also lost many when I was too slow to realise something had taken my offering.

Where fish are nymphing to the beginning of a hatch they will eventually start feeding on the surface. This can pose a problem, for so long you are fishing with your reflexes at a very fine pitch and your floating fly tends to be snatched away from the trout too soon. A trout taking down a floating fly needs several seconds grace before tightening and this timing is often upset after fishing the nymph for a while.

A very successful way of fishing the nymph is blind, casting to all the likely places and letting it drift down. A weighted nymph is usually more successful when fishing in this manner. The trout are down in the pool and that's where the artificial nymph needs to be for optimum success.

A nymph pattern fishes quite well downstream, especially in the more gravelly types of rivers. They are fished close to the bottom and allowed to drift around in a lightly controlled arc. Some of the larger woollier types of patterns are better fished in this manner, as they resemble some of the larger larvae to be found among the bottom stones such as the stonefly and creeper nymphs.

I have not given a large range of patterns here, as I feel that there are a lot of "imported" patterns that have yet to prove themselves. If they are still around in another ten years, as no doubt many of them will be, I think it can then be safely said they have found a place. Most of the successful wet and dry patterns can be tied as nymphs, and adapted in this manner they can be extremely successful.

I think that size is a very important factor and that the better results are to be obtained from smaller dressings than from some of the larger. This is especially true if the trout are taking rising nymphs. The larger sizes are better adapted for fishing close to the bottom.

BLACK GNAT NYMPH HOOK: 12–16
Tail: Black whisks
Body: Black floss
Thorax: Ostrich herl dyed black
Hackle: Black

A popular pattern derived from the wet and dry patterns.

BLACK NYMPH (No. 1) (MORRIS) HOOK: 10–12
Body: Black wool tied cigar-shape over weighted hook
Whisks: Black hen fibres
Hackle: Black

BLACK NYMPH (No. 2) (MORRIS) HOOK: 10–12
Body: Black opossum fur dubbed on weighted hook
Whisks: Black hen
Wing cases: Short tuft of black opossum fur

These patterns are the design of the late J. Morris, and are both weighted with lead wire. They sink very readily and their creator claimed that for general day fishing weighted nymphs were far deadlier than any other type.

BLACK NYMPH HOOK: 10–16
Tail: Black whisks
Body: Black floss or wool with silver wire rib
Thorax: Black wool with loose strands picked out to suggest legs
Wing cases: Pukcko wing

An excellent general pattern nymph.

BRAGG'S CADDIS LARVAE HOOK: 12–16 R. K. BRAGG
Body: Detached, made up from a mixture of golden yellow floss and a strand of yellow daylight fluorescent material

The body is built on a piece of stout nylon or gut which has been first whipped to the hook. (I dressed the pattern illustrated on a section of wing quill painted with clear lacquer)

Hackle: A small grizzle hackle which has been dyed yellowish-brown

This is R. K. Bragg's dressing for a copy of the horny-cased caddis (*Olinga (feredayi)* and should be fished close to the bottom. It is a useful pattern in comparatively shallow gravelly runs, and should be fished as an orthodox nymph.

BRAGG'S DRAGONFLY NYMPH HOOK: 8–10 R. K. BRAGG
Tail: Barred squirrel tail tied very short
Body: Fluorescent lime chenille
Hackle: Soft grizzle hackle dyed mustard and tied in palmerwise

The inventor of this pattern says that a variation, dressed with yellow chenille body, has paradoxically proved very effective during the evening beetle rise.

BROWN DRAGONFLY NYMPH   WET   HOOK: 8–12
Tail: Short tuft of black squirrel tail
Body: Brown chenille
Hackle: Brown partridge

A simple pattern of my own which is used to imitate a dragonfly larva. It should be fished as close to the bottom as possible and is used to best effect in lakes. Another pattern has a dark mossgreen body.

BROWN NYMPH   HOOK: 10–16
Tail: Brown whisks
Body: Brown floss or wool with silver rib
Thorax: Brown wool with loose strands picked out to suggest legs
Wing cases: Pheasant tail

A good general pattern.

Nymphs

CAIRN'S NYMPH (BLUE)   HOOK: 10–16
Body: Blue floss silk ribbed with silver
Thorax: Black ostrich herl
Hackle: Black

This is a popular general pattern nymph and an overseas import. There is a slight variation sometimes found dressed with a body of blue lurex tinsel.

CAIRN'S NYMPH (BLACK)   HOOK: 10–16

As CAIRN'S NYMPH (BLUE), except the body is made from black floss silk.

COACHMAN NYMPH   HOOK: 10–16
Body: Bronze peacock herl
Wing cases: White tied in beetle style
Hackle: Red

This nymph is tied slim to avoid a beetlelike appearance. Gordon Goulter tells me that the pattern is much favoured in the Wairarapa district.

DRAGONFLY KEA NYMPH   HOOK: 8–12   R. K. BRAGG
Tail: Green kea feather whisks
Body: Brown seal's fur tied plump
Wing cases: Green kea feather with tips pulled back to resemble legs
Rib: A copper wire rib is wound around body and wing cases to the head.

Another R. K. Bragg pattern that has proved its worth on back-country lakes.

EARLY SPRING OLIVE (SKUES VARIATION)   HOOK: 12–16
R. K. BRAGG

Tail: Yellowish-brown whisks
Body: Brown alive seal's fur with a little blue squirrel fur picked out at the shoulder
Rib: Gold wire

This variation of Skues's pattern is by R. K. Bragg who uses the pattern to copy the rising nymph of the spring hatches of *Leptophlebiidae*.

FURRY BLACK NYMPH   HOOK: 12–18

Tail: Black whisks
Body: Black ostrich herl with fine silver ribbing

A simple pattern that is very effective, especially in the smaller sizes.

GINGER QUILL NYMPH   HOOK: 12–16

Tail: Ginger whisks
Body: Peacock eye stripped quill
Thorax: Ginger fur from rabbit's nape
Hackle: Ginger

A useful pattern, more particularly in the smaller sizes.

GREEN AND RED   HOOK: 12–16

Body: Green
Thorax: Red
Wing cases: Hen pheasant

This is a simple little pattern that has done very well for itself in some of the Urewera streams. I'm not sure where I first came across it, but I recall that Archie Ware of Kaiangaroa does very well with it when the streams are low.

Nymphs

GREEN STONEFLY NYMPH   HOOK: 10–12
Tail: Golden pheasant tippets
Body: Olive green seal's fur ribbed with gold
Thorax: Olive seal's fur
Wing cases: Bronze peacock herl

This pattern is popular in both the northern part of the South Island and the Taranaki district. Tony Orman claims a variation of this pattern to be deadly on the Buller river. This pattern is intended to copy the stonefly larvae *Stenoperla prasina*, the green stonefly.

GREY NYMPH   HOOK: 10–16
Tail: Blue dun whisks
Body: Blue-grey wool with silver rib
Thorax: Grey wool with loose strands picked out to suggest legs
Wing cases: From the secondary feather of a mallard wing

A useful general-purpose pattern.

HARE AND COPPER NYMPH   HOOK: 10–14
Tail: Bunch of long guard hairs from a hare's pelt
Body: Dubbing of hare's fur with most of the pale hair at the roots cut off.
Wings: A tuft of hair as at the tail
Rib: Relatively heavy copper wire

Here is a killing pattern fished either in the orthodox manner with a floating line or near the bottom on a sinking line. I think that for general all-round use, when fish are not showing near or at the top, the latter method is the deadliest. I have used it successfully on many occasions.

The use of heavier copper wire serves a doublefold purpose: it forms a binding to rib the body and adds weight to take the fly down quickly. In this pattern a bunch of fibres is used for the tail. The copper is wound along the full length of the hook to the tail, where it is ribbed back to the head over a dubbing body of hare fur. Care must be taken to tease out most of the pale whiteish under-fur or the fly body will come out too pale. The body is tied relatively thin at the tail, swelling towards the shoulder with a good build-up for the thorax.

When this stage has been completed a tuft of the long guard fur from the back of the pelt is tied in at the head, suggesting perhaps the emerging wings of a nymph. Tied large and rough I have found this pattern to be very effective prior to a sedge rise. and I would expect that it presents a reasonable copy of a sedge pupa on its way to hatch. However, it is a good general pattern and I have found that summer fish schooling near the mouths of cold water creeks, often difficult to hook will take this pattern very well if it is fished very slowly along the bottom, preferably rolled along in the current with only the minimum of control from the angler.

HARE AND COPPER NYMPH (MORRIS'S)   HOOK: 10–14
J. MORRIS

Whisks: Long guard hair from a hare's pelt
Body: Dubbed hare's fur spun on a body weighted with lead wire
Rib: Copper wire

This plump-looking fly is completed with a short tuft of fur where the wing would be. Morris tied two versions of this fly, calling them the Medium and Dark. The first was of straight dubbing of hare's fur but the Dark is made of a mixture of both hare and dark opossum fur.

Mr Noel Feierabend of Dannevirke tells me that the most successful way to fish these flies is to give them a very short drift of no more than three seconds before the next cast is made. The water is quartered proceeding a step upstream every three casts or so. This is what I would call rapid-fire fishing, but apparently it is extremely successful.

HORN CADDIS NYMPH   HOOK: 10–14

Body: Grey darning wool with silver wire rib, tied down around the bend of hook and coated with clear lacquer. A narrow collar of whitish wool is tied in at the head with a few short strands of grizzle hackle to suggest the larva just protruding from the case. This pattern is fished along the bottom.

LAING'S FURRY NYMPH HOOK: 12 PETER LAING
Tail: Two whisks of the red spiny feathers at the base of a golden pheasant tail
Body: Natural ostrich herl over a base of copper wire, the end being used to rib the fly

This nymph by Peter Laing of Christchurch is considered by him to be an extremely useful general pattern. It is simple to tie and the whisks can be made from some more easily-obtained materials without affecting the usefulness of the pattern.

LAING'S QUILL HOOK: 12 PETER LAING
Tail: Brown whisks
Body and Thorax: Stripped quills from large red neck hackles
Wing cases: Cock pheasant tail

Another nymph by Peter Laing, considered by him to be an excellent pattern. He strengthens it with an application of clear cement.

LATE SPRING OLIVE (SKUES VARIATION) HOOK: 12–16
Tail: Brown-blueish fur from base of brown squirrel tail
Body: Pale brown quill of stripped peacock
Thorax: Hare's poll
Rib: Fine copper wire

R. K. Bragg ties this pattern with brown tying silk and uses it to copy the rising nymph of one of the *deleatidiums*, probably *D. Sepia*.

MARCH BROWN NYMPH HOOK: 10–16
Tail: Partridge whisks
Body: Rabbit fur with fine silver rib
Thorax: Brown rabbit nape fur
Wing cases: Brown partridge

Like its wet cousin, the March Brown nymph is a great fish catcher. It is used all over the country with equal success regardless of latitude. I have included two patterns in the coloured illustration to show how the smallest versions are often tied. The ends of the wing cases are cut off and left protruding. I have heard the opinion expressed by an angler of considerable experience that only two patterns of nymphs are needed for rising larvae, one the March Brown, the other one of the blacks.

MAYFLY NYMPH   HOOK: 12–16
Tail: Parttridge tail whisks
Body: Whiteish wool with fine silver rib
Thorax: Yellow wool
Hackle: Grey partridge
Wing cases: Brown partridge

This pattern appears to be a Bavarian one, imported to the country several years ago. It is difficult to say what species of New Zealand mayfly it might resemble, but it does take trout and seems to have found a place in many fly books.

NEW ZEALAND MAYFLY NYMPH HOOK: 10–14 R. K. BRAGG
Tail: Olive cock whisks
Body: Apple green silk covered with a strip of light green plastic
Legs: Butts of olive hackle
Wing cases: Dark speckled hen wing

This Canterbury pattern by R. K. Bragg is designed with the intention of copying the larvae of one of the mayflies, *Oniscigaster distans*.

OCTOBER BROWN   HOOK: 8–12   J. MORRIS
Tail: Two strands from cock pheasant tail
Body: Mixture of hare and opossum fur
Hackle: Dark furnace wound palmerwise along body and secured with copper rib. The fibres are then all cut short almost back to the black centre of the feather.

This pattern is the design of the late J. Morris of Bay of Plenty and was used as a deep-sunken nymph.

Nymphs

OLIVE NYMPH HOOK: 10–16
Tail: Several short gold whisks
Body: Olive wool with silver wire rib
Thorax: Mixture of olive and fawn wool
Wing cases: Bronze peacock herl

This pattern is considered by some anglers to be one of the most useful general purpose nymphs there is. Used in the smallest sizes it is deadly when fished in the orthodox manner while the larger patterns have proved themselves fished deep on a sinking line.

OPOSSUM TAIL HOOK: 12–14
Tail: Short black whisks
Body: Dubbed black fur from an opossum's tail built up to form a thorax and ribbed with silver wire

A general-purpose pattern of my own design, it has proved to be an effective evening pattern on rainbows, but I have not had a chance to use it properly on the browns. There is no reason why they should spurn it.

ORANGE NYMPH HOOK: 12–14
Tail: Short strands of brown partridge
Body: Orange wool with fine silver rib
Thorax: Rough brown wool
Wing cases: Brown partridge

This pattern is designed to represent the larva of *Zephlebia cruentata*, the New Zealand orange mayfly or the Pepper-winged olive, as Mottram called it.

PEACOCK NYMPH SERIES HOOK: 10–16
PEACOCK AND COPPER
Body: Copper wire
Thorax: Bronze peacock herl

PEACOCK AND PURPLE
Tail: Black whisks
Body: Purple floss with fine silver rib
Thorax: Bronze peacock herl

PEACOCK AND GREEN
Tail: Brown whisks
Body: Green floss with fine silver rib
Thorax: Bronze peacock herl

PEACOCK AND BLACK
Tail: Black whisks
Body: Black floss with fine silver rib
Thorax: Bronze peacock herl

PEACOCK AND RED
Tail: Natural red whisks
Body: Red floss with fine silver rib
Thorax: Bronze peacock herl

Of this series perhaps the first is the best known. It has excellent sinking qualities because of its wire body. The rest of the group can be classed as fancy patterns, but they certainly possess trout-catching qualities.

PERLA NYMPH   HOOK: 10–12
Tail: 2 cock pheasant tail strands
Body: Built up with stripped quills from long cock hackles and wound over with a large stripped quill from the eye of a peacock tail.
Wing cases: Guinea fowl
Legs: Guinea fowl and pheasant tail

This pattern is built with a dorsal-ventrally flattened body, accomplished by the use of cement during the body-building stages.

The pattern shown is a Canterbury pattern and was tied as a copy of the larvae of *Zelandoperla maculata*, the long-tailed stonefly. The pattern's name is an abbreviated form of its scientific title.

PHEASANT TAIL
Tail: Two short ends of cock pheasant tail fibres
Body: Pheasant tail fibres
Thorax: Pheasant tail fibres
Wing cases: Pheasant tail fibres

This pattern is one of the best-known nymphs on the New Zealand scene. Some anglers prefer it loaded with fine lead wire. Mr A. V. (Bruno) Kenball, the wellknown professional fly-tier of the "Red Spinner" at Hatepe, Taupo, tells me he considers it to be the best of all nymphs. Some anglers soak their patterns in clear lacquer to safeguard them. The brittle fibres of pheasant tail soon break when chewed by hapless trout.

PYE'S NYMPH   HOOK: 10–12
Body: Ginger-coloured wool tied plumpish
Hackle: Bright ginger tied sparsely and sloping back

This nymph was designed by Mr Alan Pye of the Huka Lodge on the Waikato River. It was designed to emulate the rising pupa of one of the larger sedges (*Hydropsyche Sp*) found on the Waikato River. It is used in conjunction with Pye's Waikato Sedge.

RED NYMPH   HOOK: 12–18
Tail: Grey duck wing
Body: Red silk
Thorax: Bluish rabbit fur
Hackle: Ginger
Wing cases: Grey duck wing

This pattern is especially valued in the Mataura. Mr Walter Gibb presented me with the specimen shown in the coloured plates. He considers this pattern to be the first of the set of flies for cracking the Mataura midge problem. Gibb claims that the nymph was well taken and would then be followed with an Olive Dun to imitate the sub-imago, with Welham's Red Spinner completing the trio.

RED-TIPPED GOVERNOR
Tail: Short whisks of red hackle
Body: Red
Thorax: Bronze peacock herl
Wing cases: Hen pheasant
Hackle: Red hen (optional)

A good variation of the wet and dry patterns of the same name.

SKUE'S BLUE DUN NYMPH   HOOK: 14–16
Tail: A small end of waterhen quill fibre
Body: Blue squirrel fur mixed with a touch of olive-brown seal's fur
Rib: Fine gold wire

This dressing is a slight variation of the old master's dressing, and is used by R. K. Bragg as a nymph of the hatching ephemeroptera, *Deleatidium lilli*.

TUP'S NYMPH   HOOK: 10–16
Tail: Pale ginger whisks
Body: Primrose silk
Thorax: Pink wool
Hackle: Sparse pale ginger

Highly thought of by many anglers who use it as a general-pattern nymph.

A Pastoral Stream

APPENDIX I

Identification of the members of the mayfly (Ephemeroptera) group is not always easy. That the insect is a mayfly is easily established by the angler. Anyone who has spent some time by the water will be aware of their appearance, first as a dun as it comes off the water and then as a spinner when it hovers over the water and above the pools in swarms. They prefer a still mild evening as any strong breeze will blow them away from the river.

I use a simple rule of thumb to identify them, not always with success I must admit. Having caught a specimen the first thing to observe is its size. If it is a fairly large insect with a wing span of 1¼ to 1¾ in. (32mm to 45 mm) it will be either *Ichtybotus*, *Coloburiscus* or *Oniscigaster*. In most cases there appear to be only two setae, the centre one being rudimentary. However, in the case of *Ichtybotus* the female's centre setae are longer, but still shorter than the outside pair. There is a likelihood of confusing *Oniscigaster* with *Coloburiscus* but in the case of the former the body is plump, whereas the latter is very slender.

Most anglers agree that the same set of flies will kill when trout are taking any of the above. I must confess that except for *Coloburiscus*, I have only come across sporadic hatches of the other two. That this might not be the case elsewhere.

Nesameletus is a slightly smaller fly then the preceding three. It has three short setae, the centre one reduced. Wings are about 1⅛ to 1¼ inches (28mm to 34mm).

Ameletopsis is the Kakahi Queen, recognised by the yellowish leading edge to the wings. It is very common in some districts and most anglers who have come across it are familiar with its more common name. It is about the same size as *Coloburiscus*.

The *Zephlebia* is the reclassification of the *Atalophlebia* group. These flies are difficult to distinguish from the *Deleatidium* group. All have long graceful setae, the largest, (*Z. versicolor*) having a wing span of about 1¼ inches (30mm) while the smallest (*D. Cerinum*) are about half-inch (12mm). I have seen some unidentifiable species that appeared to be even smaller than this.

Even the scientists have difficulty in identifying species without the aid of magnification, so the amateur naturalist can only hope to identify groups with recourse to authoritative references — and even these do not always agree. I have omitted giving colouration as I have found this to be confusing. Often a colour will be but a subtle hint and on occasions I have found a standard description based on colour to be downright misleading. For the purposes of the angler I think the foregoing will be an aid. Selected references are mentioned in the acknowledgments at the beginning of the book.

APPENDIX II

This appendix is devised by the Christchurch fly dresser and angler, Robert K. Bragg, based on his field notes and observation of nature's law of colouration and the influence it has in the design of artificial flies intended to imitate those insects encountered by the New Zealand angler.

Given here is the scientific name of the insect, its common name (if any) and the pattern of artificial fly intended to imitate the creature in each phase of its cycle, where this concerns both the trout and the angler. The time of the year the insect is to be found is designated by one or more letters. E is for early (October, November) M & L, middle and late (December–May), and L, late (April, May).

This table is intended merely as a guide. Its author admits that there are many other patterns which could serve equally well, but those nominated by him were, at the time of compilation, the ones he favoured most. The reader will notice many gaps in the Ephemeridae nymph group. This is to be understood as by the time a hatching species has been identified the dun is already emerging and a floating fly is called for. Besides this, there are several nymph patterns that appear to be taken by the trout for several species and most anglers agree that the same pattern, if of the right size, will serve them well at most times.

Where more than one fly is given to represent a species, this is to allow for seasonal and geographical colour variations within a species.

MAYFLIES

	INSECT	ARTIFICIAL FLY	ARTIFICIAL NYMPH
E	Ichthybotus hudsoni	Mottram's Mayfly Dun	N.Z. Mayfly Nymph
		Mottram's Mayfly Spinner	
E	Leptophlebiidae family	Bragg's early Olive Dun	Early spring olive
L	Zephlebia nodularis	Dad's Favourite	
M & L	Zephlebia cruentata	Pepper-winged Olive Dun	Orange Nymph
M & L	Zephlebia dentata	Kakahi Queen	
E. & L	Deleatidium lilli	Brer Rabbit — Blue Dun — Red Fox	
E	Deleatidium myzobranchia	Studholme's Greenwell	Hare's Ear
M & L	Coloburiscus humeralis	Twilight Beauty	Kite's Brown
M & L	Ameletopsis percitus	Nilsen's Churchill — Kakahi Queen	Kite's Brown
L	Deleatidium sepia	Minson's Fancy	
L	Deleatidium versicolor	Brer Fox	

STONEFLIES

M & L	Zelandoperla maculata	New Zealand Stonefly	Perla Nymph

GRASSHOPPER

M & L	Aucklandobius trivacuata	Dean's Grasshopper	

CADDIS

	Olinga Feredayi		Horny-cased Caddis
	Triplectides Obsoleta	Caddis Fly	Nilsen's Maggot Caddis
			Caddis Larvae

BEETLES

E & M	Costelytra zealandica (Brown beetle)	Coch-y-bondhu	
E & M	Pyronota festiva (Green beetle)	West Coast Beetle — Love's Lure	

DRAGON AND DAMSEL FLIES

M & L	Xanthocnemis zealandica (Red Damsel fly)	Tonga — Danielson's Damsel	Bragg's Dragon Nymph
	Muscidae	Blue Bottle — Black Gnat — Dean's Black Gnat	

APPENDIX III

Listed below are those tiers who were responsible for some of the patterns included in the coloured plates.

PLATE 1
The late Bernard Fletcher   Spa Special
O.S. (Budge) Hintz   Parson's Glory original tie

PLATE 2
The late Bernard Fletcher   Craig's Night time
R. K. Bragg   Hope's White   Yellow Terror
   Yellow Bully   Mrs Simpson Kea
   Hope's Dark   Sweep
   Hart's Creek   Red Shadow
   Red Brunton   Yellow Terror
John Cockburn   Jock Miller
Peter Laing   Orange Witch
Walter Willis   Buggs Bunny   Hilda

PLATE 3
R. K. Bragg   Bragg's Dragon Nymph   Perla Nymph
Peter Laing   Laing's Quill Nymph   Laing's Furry Nymph
Noel Thomas   Te Muka

PLATE 4
The late J. (Jimmy) Morris   Black Palmer   Summer Dun
   Green and Brown Beetles
The late Lester Welham   Welham's Red Spinner
R. K. Bragg   Hunt's Favourite   Brer Rabbit
   Bragg's Blue Dun
Walter Willis   Lacemoth

The rest of the flies were either tied by myself or from my collection.

BIBLIOGRAPHY

Books which I used for reference and which I recommend to my readers are:

A Dictionary of Trout Flies, by A. Courtney-William, Black, London

Field Notes for the Freshwater Naturalist, by P. Dickinson Dominion Museum Handbook No. 3)

Fisherman's Country, by G. F. Hobbs, Bles, London.

The Flies In My Hat, by G. G. Kelly, Hodder & Stoughton, Auckland.

Fly Dressers' Guide, by John Veniard, Black, London.

Fly Fishing In New Zealand, by George Ferris, Heinemann, London.

An Introduction to the Freshwater Insects of New Zealand, by J. C. Prendergast and D. R. Cowley, Collins, Auckland.

Native and Introduced Freshwater Fishes, by C. S. Woods, A. H. and A. W. Reed Wellington.

Native Fishes of New Zealand, by W. J. Phillipps, A. H. and A. W. Reed, Wellington.

New Zealand Fishing and Shooting Gazette (ceased publication).

New Zealand Outdoor Magazine.

Rising Fish, by R. Dickinson, Whitcombe & Tombs, Christchurch.

Trout Fising and Sport in Maoriland, by Captain G. D. Hamilton, New Zealand Government Printer, Wellington.

GLOSSARY OF TERMS

Abdomen: The stomach or rear portion of an insect's body. In nymph dressing, the rear half of the body is referred to as the abdomen.
Antennae: The feelers of an insect.
Bi-visible: A palmer style of fly with the front portion of the hackle tied with a white hackle.
Bronze mallard: The dark copper-coloured scapular feathers of a mallard drake.
Coverts: The small feathers on top of a bird's wings are called the top coverts. The Leslie's Lure is often tied with these feathers from a hen pheasant. The under coverts are located beneath the wing.
Detached body: Occasionally used in making some mayflies and also damsel flies. The method is used to imitate a long body without resorting to an over-long hook which would increase the weight of a floating fly.
Dropper: A short length of nylon or gut attached to a cast from which a fly is suspended. It was once customary to fish with several droppers but this custom has almost disappeared.
Dry fly: A fly which is normally dressed with stiff hackles on a light hook. It is annointed with an oil-based floatant and fished with a floating line. The fly is intended to copy an insect floating on the surface of the water.
Dubbing: A mixture of fur or wool which is spun on a thread and then wound around the hook to form a fly's body.
Dun: An angler's term, used to denote a freshly-hatched insect of the Ephemeroptera (mayfly) order as it floats down a stream. Scientific name Imago.
Elytra: See Wing cases.
Ephemeroptera: The order of insects commonly known as mayflies.
Fall of spinners: When adult insects of the mayfly family are drifting spent upon the water.
Fancy Fly: A Hardy's Favourite is known as a fancy fly. It is not intended to copy any particular insect.
Flank feathers: The large body feathers to be found below a bird's wing.
Floss: The name for the silk used in dressing bodies of flies.
Fluorescent: Some body materials such as chenille and yarn are dyed with very intense colours. One of the earliest yarns was known as gatron. Red, lime, yellow and orange are the most favoured colours.
Gallena: The spotted plumage of the guinea fowl.
Gatron: See fluorescent.
Grey drake: The grey body plumage of a mallard drake.
Hackle: The feather used to wind around the head of a fly. It serves several purposes. It was originally used to copy the legs of an insect. It can be used to suggest wings and in the case of a dry fly it serves to stand the fly up on the water. Soft feathers are usually used for wet flies or lures, while stiff sparkly feathers are used for dry flies. These fall into several categories. They can be the soft breast feathers of such birds as partridge but are normally from the neck of domestic poultry. These may be either cock or hen, the latter being only suitable for wet flies. Those from the neck of a bird are called neck hackles and these are used for dry flies in the small sizes while the larger are favoured for making lures. A short rounded hackle with stiff barbs is found on the back

and these are called spade hackles. The long tapered ones that droop down each side of the body ahead of a rooster's tail are called saddle hackles. We are primarily concerned with neck hackles but all three come in a great variety of colours and patterns. Black, white, grey and the artificially dyed ones are obvious, but some of the fancy and highly prized variations need some description.

Badger. A white or creamy feather with a black centre.

Barred Rock. Also known as grizzle. These hackles come from the Plymouth Rock breed.

Blue Dun. These occur but rarely in nature and nearly all flies are tied with dyed feathers. A proper blue dun is a blueish-grey feather with golden dun flecks in the points.

Coch-y-bondhu. A natural red feather with a black centre and black tips used in tying a Coch-y-bondhu fly. This term however has come to be used when describing this type of hackle which is really a style of furnace hackle.

Cree. Coloured grizzle, usually with touches of ginger mixed with the black and grey.

Furnace. A natural red or ginger feather with a black centre. The ginger type is often called a greenwell after the fly it is used to dress.

Ginger. A pale red to golden colour.

Gizzle. As barred rock.

Honey Dun. A pale light brown feather with yellowish gold tints.

Honey Grizzle. A pale golden feather patched with darker gold or blueish-grey markings. Sometimes it will be a pale buff colour. This feather is often called a Parsons after the Parson's Glory lure which is dressed with it.

Red (natural). A feather which may range from copper to a deep brick red.

Sussex. A white or cream feather lightly flecked with black.

Hackle fly: One is which no wings are used, only a hackle being wound around the head.

Hackle point wings: The tips of feathers used to represent the wings of an insect — usually a spent mayfly.

Halford F.M.: Considered to be the father of dry fly angling, Halford perfected his art on the chalk streams of Southern England. In 1886 he published *Floating Flies and How to Dress Them*, and so began the cult that became so restricted by dogma that anglers were driven into opposing camps of theory. He will be remembered as one of the prophets of angling so long as there are trout left to cast to.

Hatch: When a large number of a species of insect is upon the water it is referred to as a "hatch". Used correctly it should only describe the emergence of those insects which spend their larval stages underwater, such as mayflies, sedges, etc.

Head: The part of a fly where all the bits and pieces are finally tied in, whipped and then covered with a varnish or lacquer.

Heavy dressing: When a fly is dressed in such a way as to form a bulky fly it is referred to as being heavily dressed. Many Canterbury lures fit this description.

Herl: The strands that form the tail feathers of such birds as peacock and ostrich. A strip is wound around a hook to form fly bodies.

Imago: See Dun.

Jungle Cock: This is a breed of wildfowl that inhabits the jungles of India and Asia. The cock bird has a neck of feathers that appear to be covered with an enamel-like substance and have an "eye" at the end of each feather. These are used extensively for dressing salmon flies and many New Zealand lures but

they are now protected by law in most countries and are almost unobtainable.
Kip: A trade name given to calf tails.
Larvae: The first stage of insect development.
Lure: A general term which might be used to describe any artificial concoction used to catch trout, but more specifically it is used to describe a large wet fly of the type used in Taupo, Canterbury and Rotorua, which imitates a fish rather than an insect.
Lurex: A modern material of a shiny metallic appearance used in fly dressing.
Mayfly: This term is generally used to cover all members of the Ephemeroptera group. While it is not really correct it has, through common use, become an accepted form of definition.
Mylar: A type of metallic-looking plastic which when braided in a piping form is used to make the body of streamer flies.
Nape: The back of an animal's neck. Some furs from this part are used specifically.
Nondescript: A type of fly designed to cover the general aspects of a group of insects without specifically copying any one species.
Nymphs: The larval form of underwater insects. Some pupating insects (namely caddis) are also referred to as nymphs. As an angling term, it is applied to any insect which is in the act of rising to the surface prior to hatching in the adult form.
Opossum: The Australian marsupial phalanger which was introduced to New Zealand is now widely spread. Its fur is used by some fly dressers.
Pale watery: A visual description of some members of the mayfly group.
Palmer: (Palmer fashion). A style of fly made by winding hackles along the length of the hook shank. Many flies are hackled in this manner and are referred to as being tied palmer-fashion, or palmer-wise.
Parachute flies: The hackle is wound on an upright projection from the shoulder of the hook. This allows the fly to settle very gently on the surface where the body of the fly rides lower in the water than with a conventional dry fly.
Paradise duck: A species (Tadorna variegata) indigenous to New Zealand. The plumage of this bird is prized by some fly tiers.
Peacock plumage: The tail feathers are mainly used, the most common being the bronze centre plumes, the herl of which is used for many wet and dry flies. The green sword tail feathers are also used, but to a lesser extent. The eye of a bronze feather is used to obtain the quills used in making quill-bodied flies.
Primaries: The long flight feathers in a bird's wing.
Pupae: A stage of metamorphosis through which some insects pass before hatching in adult form.
Quill bodies: Those bodies made from a strip from the eye of a peacock's tail. The short herl is rubbed off, the strip of quill wrapped around the hook to simulate the segments of an insect's body. With some patterns other feathers are used.
Rib or ribbing: The wire or tinsel wound over the body of a fly.
Rough dressing: Some flies are deliberately dressed in a shaggy manner to give a calculated rough appearance. This is not to be confused with an untidy fly which has been poorly tied.
Scapulas: The broad feathers next to the body on the top of a bird's wing.
Secondaries: Those feathers between the scapular and flight primaries of a bird's wing. In the case of the duck families these feathers are iridescent.
Setae: The whisks at the tail of an insect. In the case of some families such as the mayfly group, these are very long.
Skues, G.E.M.: An English angler who was a contemporary of Halford. Skues

is recognised as being the father of applied nymph fishing and his publication, *Minor Tactics of a Chalk Stream* published in 1910 fully described this art. He is better known, however, for his second book *The Way of a Trout With a Fly*, a careful study of the habits of brown trout and the manner in which they feed. His theories at the time were regarded in some quarters as being heretical. It is my opinion that his works are of more practical use to a New Zealand angler than are the writings of Halford, which are rather narrow in scope and application.

Slim dressing: A very light application of hackle and wing to a fly so that it has a slender appearance in the water. This applies particularly to lures.

Special: A term used to describe a dressing which is regarded as being exclusive to a person or retailer, more usually the latter. The term "special" often denotes an aura of deadliness that is sometimes unwarranted.

Speculae: The iridescent secondary feathers in a duck's wing.

Spider fly: A softly-hackled wet fly — not usually intended to represent a spider.

Spinner: The imago, or final adult form of a mayfly.

Spoonbill: The New Zealand shoveller duck (*Anas rhynchotis*).

Stewart, R. C.: Author of *The Practical Angler*, published in 1857. Stewart, who fished the border country between Scotland and England, settled forever the dispute over upstream and downstream angling with wet flies, proving beyond doubt the obvious advantages of the former.

Streamer fly: An American term which when used properly, denotes a large wet fly or lure with a long wing intended to copy, more or less, a small fish. Many of our New Zealand lures come into this category although there is the difference that we, unlike the Americans, secure the wing to the body with a tinsel ribbing.

Sub-imago: The dun of a mayfly. From the second moulting emerges the spinner, or imago.

Tag: A small tuft of wool, usually red, or a short turn of floss or tinsel at the end of a fly body.

Tail: In a lure this can be of squirrel tail or coloured whisks. In wet or dry flies a bunch of whisks or golden pheasant tippet is used. Sometimes hair may be used.

Teals: The flank feathers of a teal duck. These are imported.

Tippets: Black-tipped orange fibres from the neck of a male golden pheasant. They are used extensively in wet fly patterns.

Thorax: The middle section of an insect to which the wings and legs are attached.

Topping: Used in salmon flies and some Canterbury lures. It may be golden pheasant crest or green peacock sword herl.

Variant: A dry fly dressed with very long hackles.

Wet fly: Any fly which is fished under the surface of the water.

Whisks: Fibres from a cock's hackle used to copy the setae of an insect.

Wing cases: The hard wing coverings or elytra of a beetle.